Fiona Gall

Critical Issues in Religious Education

EDITED BY OLIVER BRENNAN

VERITAS

First published 2005 by
Veritas Publications
7/8 Lower Abbey Street
Dublin 1
Ireland
Email publications@veritas.ie
Website www.veritas.ie

ISBN 1 85390 652 2

A catalogue record for this book is available from the British Library.

Cover design by Colette Dower
Printed in the Republic of Ireland by Betaprint Ltd., Dublin

*Veritas books are printed on paper made from the wood pulp of managed
forests. For every tree felled, at least one tree is planted, thereby renewing
natural resources.*

Contents

Contributors

Dr Oliver Brennan has completed post-graduate studies in Education and Church Leadership at Fordham University, New York, where he is currently an adjunct professor. He is the author of numerous articles as well as *Cultures Apart? The Catholic Church and Contemporary Irish Youth* (Veritas, 2001). He is parish priest of Haggardstown, Blackrock, Dundalk, Co. Louth.

Dr Finola Cunnane is Director of Religious Education in the Diocese of Ferns, Wexford. She has completed post-graduate studies at Fordham University, New York and lectures with the Mater Dei Institute of Education, Dublin City University, on the School Chaplaincy Programme. She contributes to many journals and is the author of *New Directions in Religious Education* (Veritas, 2004).

Dr Kieran Scott is a Professor of Religious Education at Fordham University, New York. He is the author of numerous articles in the field of religious education as well as co-editor of *Perspectives on Marriage* (2nd Edition Oxford University Press, 2000). He completed his post-graduate studies at Columbia University, New York. His expertise is in adult education, curriculum theory and systematic theology.

Prologue

One of the great challenges facing the world at the dawn of the twenty-first century is the provision of quality religious education. In an era characterised by globalisation, counter-globalisation, established versus fundamentalist religion and, above all the clash between the Islamic and Christian civilisations, the provision of authentic, high quality religious education and properly trained teachers is of immeasurable importance. A growing awareness of this new challenge is reflected in a recent analysis of the situation in the British schooling system, which pointed to the need for very significant improvements in the content and quality of the religious education syllabus as well as in the adequate training of competent religious educators.[1]

An Interim Report agreed by the European Council and Commission on 26 February 2004, at a meeting chaired by the then Irish Minister for Education, Mr Noel Dempsey, reflected the strategic importance now accorded by the European Community to the teaching profession as it faces the challenges of the knowledge society. This coincides with similar concerns of the OECD when it stated recently; 'Making teaching more attractive for both present and future teachers becomes a more urgent policy concern'.[2] It points to the importance of recognition, professional development and shared ethos which is as relevant for practicing teachers as it is for potential recruits. To help achieve this, the OECD has launched a major study in twenty-seven countries, including Ireland, which is due to be completed by the end of 2004. According to Professor John Coolahan, 'This new priority being given to the teaching career by such major international bodies signals a realisation of the centrality of the teaching force as a mediating agency for society as it now grapples with major social, economic and cultural change'.[3]

In an era of such unforeseen, profound and accelerating economic, social and cultural change, the role of the education system and the centrality of religious education within that system, becomes crucially important. While teachers' morale, motivation, competence and commitment have always been of importance, it has never been more urgent than in our contemporary and emerging cultural reality. 'In the context of the contemporary knowledge society, teaching and learning now take centre stage'.[4] Teaching, whether at home, in the local community, or in the school setting is one of the great humane professions as it helps to nurture, support and develop learners of all ages. The engagement of teacher and participant in the pursuit of learning enriches humanity and is now, more than ever, a noble pursuit. In a culture which requires life-long learning, the teacher of today must above all others be a life-long learner.[5]

The narrow understanding of the aim of religious education which confines it to that of nurturing faith is no longer viable. This is but one, and only one, dimension of the important field of religious education. A major contribution that one can make to the establishment of right relations among peoples within nations and between the nations of the world is through the exploration of the wider meaning of religious education.

This book attempts to begin a conversation in this regard. The beginning of any conversation around a vital task requires a two-fold concentration. Firstly, we need to examine the context, that is, map the territory of the journey into the unknown. Secondly, before setting out on any journey, we need to know where we want to go; we need a vision. The journey of exploration into the activity of religious education requires good leadership, and leadership without a worthy ethical vision is not only useless, but dangerous and destructive.

It has become painfully obvious, as a result of recent world atrocities, that religious understanding significantly determines attitudes and actions towards other peoples and nations. Religion identifies a culture, and cultural understanding can be a matter of life or death. It is hoped that the important conversation that is initiated by the authors of this book will become a transnational and global pursuit. As Heidegger once said, 'To recognise a frontier is to already have gone beyond it'. True learning stretches the heart as well as the mind and the right question is often more valuable than the easy answer.

Oliver Brennan

1 February 2005

Notes

1. Report on BBC TV April 2004
2. Report in *The Irish Times*, March 26, 2004
3. John Coolahan, *Making Progress in Education: A Special Report*, The Irish Times: March 26, 2004
4. Ibid.
5. Ibid.

Introduction

A conversation on this book began in October 2001 at a seminar in Mater Dei Institute of Education, Dublin, which was organised by the Religion Teachers' Association of Ireland and Mater Dei. In the context of a vigorous creative conversation very significant issues emerged. This conversation has been considerably developed by the contributors to this book and offers a helpful contribution to what is hoped will be a continuing dialogue.

Chapter One sets the context for the conversation – a post-modern culture with a plurality of sensibilities. Gaining a deeper insight into this culture is a pre-requisite to recognising the importance of the settings of religious education as well as what it means to engage in religious education.

Chapter Two is an attempt to unveil the richest meaning of religious education. Recognising that this activity is central to human life, Dr Finola Cunnane argues that religious education is an indispensable endeavour. She calls for a new theory of religious education and suggests that we turn to education as an overall framework for this task. Drawing on the seminal insights of Gabriel Moran she stresses the importance of embracing the two aims of religious education, namely, teaching people religion with all the depth and breadth of intellectual excitement and teaching people to be religious in all the very concrete ways that show us the way to the fullness of life.[1]

Chapter Three attempts to uncover the meaning of 'to teach religion'. While acknowledging that social and cultural forces are vital components to consider in every educational context, Dr Kieran Scott examines the issues from the perspective of the teacher, or more precisely from the side of the act of teaching. He explores the meaning of the verb 'to teach' and its object 'religion' as they intermingle, interplay and intersect in contemporary schooling.

Having made a strong case for the teaching of religion, Kieran Scott is convinced that schools alone cannot bear the entire burden and challenge of religious education, not least because this system would be inadequate for a full, intelligent religious life. Schooling needs to be reinforced by other diverse and complementary forms of religiously educative activities. The challenge ahead then, is to place schooling in religion in a larger context of complementary educational forms of life.

Considering the currents of post-modernity that have disturbed the Irish cultural waters, with the consequent rebellion of young people against inherited religious embodiment, Scott calls for the opening up of new and flexible tracts to access their lives. As well as claiming some of the richer elements of its own Celtic religious past, the Irish religious community could benefit from the incorporation of some of the United States and British forms and practices of religious education. What is selectively adopted from these foreign sources could be combined with a distinctive Irish past and with present post-modern sensibilities. Chapter Four addresses the pivotal issue of how to place the practice and study of religion in balanced interaction with each other in our contemporary milieu.

In Chapter 5, Dr Scott demonstrates how a post-modern re-interpretation of the classic doctrine of the Trinity can have profound ethical, spiritual, political and educational implications for the practice of a transformed religious way of life in a parish.

Oliver Brennan
1 February 2005

Notes

1. G. Moran, *Understanding Religion and Being Religious* (1992) p.252.

Chapter 1

The Cultural Context for Religious Education Today

OLIVER BRENNAN

It is my conviction that the better we understand the culture of our time and our place the more effective we will be in whatever role we have in life. This chapter takes a brief look at the changing shape of culture and how best to respond and interact with this new reality as a community of faith.

A key factor hampering the influence and effectiveness of religious institutions today is their failure to pay attention to, and deepen their understanding of, contemporary culture. The importance of this is highlighted in the words of a young person arising out of recent research.

> During my time at the university in Dublin, my perception of religion became increasingly negative. I was now immersed in a whole new culture that bore little or no similarity to the culture of my childhood and adolescence.[1]

If our parenting, teaching and pastoral ministry is to have a significant influence on culture, its forms and directions, and on the individual's response to one's ambient culture, we need to gain some understanding of the history, conclusions and attitudes of the new sciences, as well as contemporary philosophical understandings and perspectives. The work of *[handwritten margin note:]* Going back and not considering the make up of country

Even in Catholic schools not all students are

need to consider young people background → some have very little

...clear that people's ...al social origins. As ...provides the stuff ...ich conscious life ...shaping tendency of ...at the process of ...erson and his or her

...cur, they inevitably ...and since culture ...it is essential to ...iate how it affects religious belief and practice. In particular, as Michael Warren notes, 'the situation of young people cannot be properly understood without attention to how social and cultural forces affect them'.[4] Indeed, according to Tom Beaudoin there is a profound symbiosis between young people and popular culture: '[young people] cannot be understood apart from popular culture, and much of popular culture cannot be interpreted without attention to [young people]'.[5] Contemporary lived culture shapes the meaning systems and values of the rising generation. An important dimension of religious education concerns meanings and values.

What is Culture?

When one examines literature on the topic of culture over the past century and a half it becomes clear that the understanding of this concept has changed dramatically during that period of time. The classical notion of culture is best defined by Matthew Arnold in the middle of the nineteenth century. For him, culture was the preserve of the elite. A 'cultured person' was one who leaned towards the aesthetic and strived for excellence. He or she rose above the mechanical and material civilisation of the industrial age. These people were usually found in the world of academia and the arts. During and after

Arnold's time the concept of culture began to expand, but it was not until the first half of the twentieth century that the term 'culture' was given a much wider meaning by anthropologists and sociologists. Instead of the strong or almost exclusive association of this concept with the artistic and the intellectual, the idea of culture was becoming synonymous with a way of life. Today it is generally accepted that 'culture constitutes a total context that shapes us all'.[6] We create our culture and our own creation influences us deeply. In this regard, Clifford Geertz makes an apt comment. The human being is 'an animal suspended in webs of significance he himself has spun'.[7] These webs of significance constitute culture. Geertz's understanding of culture includes the crucial roles of symbols as carriers of culture and this is of particular significance in regard to the dynamic interplay of culture and religious faith.

This brief outline of the evolution in the understanding of culture shows that the definition of the concept has changed significantly in the past century, paralleling in its evolution the increasing importance ascribed by sociologists, anthropologists, philosophers and other scholars to culture as the dominant factor in the internal and external relationships of any society. The findings of critical history put an end to the classical assumptions that understood culture in a narrow, unitarian manner, a normative view of culture that, according to Shorter, 'inhibited the Church's missionary activity' and 'distorted the Church's own understanding of itself'.[8] It is now generally accepted that the manner in which people experience reality, especially the young, is culture-bound. Since culture is a developing process rather than a static entity and since authentic religious faith can only exist in a cultural form, there needs to be continuous dialogue between religious faith and culture.

In considering the impact of culture on religious belief and practice, it is important to note its historical dimension, one of the six categories identified by Kroeber and Kluckhohn.[9] In this regard, Alyward Shorter comments that 'culture is... essentially a transmitted pattern of meanings embodied in symbols, a pattern capable of development and change, and it belongs to the concept of humanness itself.'[10] It follows that since religion is a divine-human phenomenon, it inevitably affects, and is affected by, culture. Because of the historical dimension and because by its nature culture seeks to pass on its cumulative wisdom from one generation to the next, an inherited culture can be severely challenged during a period of rapid social change. What has occurred in Ireland in recent decades is a good illustration of this phenomenon.

The Nature of Contemporary Culture
The cultural context in which we live today is variously described as high modernity, late modernity, post-modernity, and, most recently, the era of globalisation. Before examining the reality in which we live and work today it is valuable to examine briefly the causes of cultural change. Cultural change begins with economic change, that is, change in the ways and means of production. What has happened in Ireland over the last few decades is a microcosm of what has happened, and will happen, anywhere in the world. The economic changes that have occurred in Ireland in a period of two decades spanned one hundred years in Great Britain, Western Europe and the United States. An examination of the Irish reality, therefore, sets out in sharp relief the effects of this phenomenon wherever it may occur.

In 1958, when the programme for economic expansion was launched, few people could have imagined the extraordinary impact it would have on a small island perched in the Atlantic Ocean off the west coast of Europe. The end result of this change is that the Republic of Ireland is now one of the largest exporters of information technology in the world, followed closely by the United States and is ranked as the most 'globalised' country among sixty-two states included in the annual A T Kearney Foreign Policy Magazine Survey.[11]

Economic change always leads to social change, that is, change in the ways in which people live, an example of which is the revolution in the ways of communication. The change from a predominantly rural population to a largely urban-based concentration of people brings huge demographic shifts with all the social consequences that follow. The result is that the urban nuclear family becomes estranged from its rural roots in family and community.

Cultural change always follows economic and social change, but whereas the latter two forms of change can be measured in GNP, GDP or demographic shifts, the former cannot be so easily understood or perceived. Economic and social change occur at the level of observable data, whereas cultural change occurs beneath the surface of what can be seen and measured. Cultural change concerns meanings and values and it is this type of change (not economic and social change per se) that affects both religious beliefs and values.

The movement through economic, social and cultural change parallels the progression from pre-modernity to modernity and finally into post-modernity. This phenomenon becomes clear by briefly examining it in microcosmic form in the Irish context. As one moves through the latter decades of the last century Ireland progressed from pre-modernity, rapidly through modernity into a post-modern culture.

The pre-modern world is characterised by a very hierarchical society where authority is respected, especially religious authority. Metaphysically, it is characterised by an adherence to universals and absolutes: a particular truth is always and everywhere true, irrespective of what an individual feels or thinks. Pre-modern morality emphasises duty and obligation in order to reproduce the established order. Church language betrays this, for example, in the use of the term 'holydays of obligation'. This is reflected in the comments of a contemporary young man who is committed to the Church:

> Young people of my age tend to think that what is right or wrong depends on each person. I would have a certain sympathy for their point of view, but I believe that there are certain moral standards to be upheld and that there is an actual right or wrong irrespective of what individual people think. I would not go along with the old idea that 'black is black' and 'white is white', but I do believe in holding on to certain objective standards.[12]

Modernity is characterised by individualism. This has replaced the strong sense of community that was characteristic of the pre-modern world: 'I'll do my own thing in my own way irrespective of what anyone else thinks or says'. According to Charles Taylor, the individualism of modernity is mainly characterised by the permissive society, narcissism and the 'me' generation. He says that the atomism of the self-absorbed individual militates against participation in different levels of government as well as in voluntary organisations. Another strong feature of modernity concerns the primacy of instrumental reason, that is 'the kind of rationality we draw on when we calculate the most economical application of means to a given end'[13] without also taking into account the moral implications. This is demonstrated in the closing down of profitable industries in order to maximise profit. Instrumental reason can also be used in a manner that can be highly destructive, for example, the failure to prevent global warming resulting in the destruction of the ozone layer.

Taylor says that the moral ideal of self-fulfilment or authenticity, which is at the heart of modernity, should not be implicitly discredited because of its debased and deviant forms. However, I believe that a purely personal understanding of self-fulfilment has a significant negative impact on Christian faith.

Life in community is central to the understanding of discipleship. This is a core dimension of Christian faith. In the Judeo-Christian tradition, God's self-communicating revelation was always to a community or to an individual-in-community and it invited a community response. The early Church was particularly conscious of Christian faith lived-in-community as is evidenced in the Acts of the Apostles and other writings. Because the culture of authenticity, which is a constituent part of modernity, encourages a very personal understanding of self-fulfilment, it is, according to Taylor, 'antithetical to any strong commitment to community'.[14] When one does enter into community it tends to be for instrumental reasons. This mentality has been a particular challenge to a religious belief system built around community.

High Modernity, Late Modernity, Post-Modernity or Globalisation

How can the culture of our time and place best be described? It is essential to name contemporary reality in order to better understand it. Much discussion has taken place around this question over the past number of years. Some commentators argue that we are still in the era of modernity. However, most philosophers, theologians, sociologists, anthropologists and educators believe that humankind has moved beyond the strictly modern era. Michael Paul Gallagher, for example, traces the death of modernity and the birth of post-modernity to the fall of the Berlin Wall in 1989. It seems to me that while this may be true in an ideological sense, one cannot easily ascribe an exact date to this cultural shift. While one recognises that this event symbolised the end of one cultural epoch, contemporary Western culture continues to be characterised by elements of modernity as well as post-modernity. While there was a clean break between the cultural realities of pre-modernity and that of modernity, this was not the case regarding the movement from modernity to post-modernity. A major dyke arose between the river of pre-modernity and modernity whereas the river of modernity flows freely into the sea of post-modernity.

Most religious educators across North America and Canada date the origins of post-modernity to the early 1960s, particularly as it affects young people. There is general agreement that Western culture is passing through a paradigm shift and this cultural movement is generally referred to as 'post-modernism' or 'post-modernity'. Leuze suggests that since we live in a transitional, developing period, the term 'post-modern', though nebulous, is appropriate 'since that which has not yet happened can only be descried by what has happened'.[15]

Nancy Murphy states that a holistic epistemology, which is characteristic of post-modernism has no foundational element, so that 'justification of a problematic belief involves showing connections with beliefs held to be unproblematic'.[16] Whereas the philosophy of modernism depended on a foundational statement for validity, a holistic epistemology discovers its strength in the relationship between beliefs. Gill gives further clarification to this perspective by stating that in the modern context 'knowledge is... an essentially static relationship between the knower's mind and the outside world'.[17] Sorri and Gill also point out that 'knowledge has almost always been construed exclusively in terms of the mind, as if those who engage in cognitive activity do so completely apart from bodily activity'.[18] In other words, a non-contextualised, disembodied epistemology was characteristic of modernism. Gill states that in post-modern epistemology 'knowing is something persons do.... There is no knowledge apart from knowers'.[19] Truth is a dynamic process which human beings experience. It is contextualised and embodied in particular situations by particular people.

Modern knowledge is understood in an atomistic manner in the sense that there is a foundational belief from which other beliefs may infer justification. In considering knowledge holistically, post-modern epistemology, as Leuze points out, either 'does not address individual beliefs or it does so with the recognition that they are interrelated with other beliefs and that the system is not reducible. The focus is on the system of beliefs rather than on individual tenets of belief'.[20]

The implications of this epistemological understanding for religious education, according to Leuze, are that 'the resulting model either will be constructed of consistent parts (a systemic model) or there will be an awareness of the tensions between inconsistent parts'.[21] Another characteristic of modern and post-modern epistemologies that has significant implications for Christian faith, particularly in its Catholic embodiment, is the relationship of a belief system to varying viewpoints. For the modern epistemologist there are absolutes, since truth can exist apart from the knower, and the holding of differing viewpoints suggests error. In contrast, post-modern epistemology lauds diversity as a reflection of the diversity of contexts rather than viewing it as an indicator of erroneous viewpoints. Aronowitz and Giroux support an epistemology 'in which different voices and traditions exist and flourish to the degree that they listen to the voices of others... and maintain those conditions in which the act of communicating and living extends rather than restricts the creation of democratic public life.'[22]

In seeking uniformity of belief with its attendant view of disembodied truth, modern epistemology had a comfortable home in the Catholic Church and in other established religious systems. Post-modern epistemology, with its affirmation of diversity, presents a new challenge.

The post-modern philosophical understanding of language as a communal achievement contrasts with that of modernism which saw it, rather, in terms of a collection of individuals' achievements. This is similar to Vygotsky's psychological explanation of the acquisition of language, wherein thought and language are first socially shaped and then individually possessed.[23] In the view of Leuze 'the import of this for religious language is also a communal task rather than an individual task'.[24]

Murphy says that a post-modern 'non-individualist or "corporate" view of community' is replacing the individualism and atomism of modernism.[25] However, post-modern belief in what Murphy calls a 'renewed sense of the importance and irreducibility of community' does not deny the significance of the individual; rather, the conception is that the individual cannot be understood apart from his or her role in the community.[26] Bronfenbrenner's ecological psychology would extend this thinking by claiming that the individual can only be understood in terms of the complex network of microsystems and ecosystems of which he or she is part within macrosystems.[27] Since post-modernists understand community interactively and organically, Leuze says that 'an implication of this characteristic for religious education is the recognition that the religious community (like a holistic epistemology) is a web of interrelated elements'.[28] While affirming individual significance, this is to be understood in relationship with other community members.

The post-modernist appreciation of the importance of the irreducibility of community stands in stark contrast to Taylor's description of atomistic modernism. While not engaging this dimension of post-modern thought, it is important to keep in mind that contemporary culture is still characterised by an individualism that tends to see fulfilment as just of the self, 'neglecting or delegitimating the demands that come from beyond our own desires or aspirations, be they from history, tradition, society, nature or God', leading to a radical anthropocentrism and social atomism.[29]

As post-modernism's fresh understanding of, and emphasis on, community filters down to lived contemporary culture, it appears to augur well for a religious faith that is community based. Thus, Christian Churches and other community-based religious faiths should benefit greatly from this dimension of post-modernity. However, this will be determined by the model of Church or religious institution that is operative. As Leuze points out, 'in the post-modern perspective, hierarchies are levelled and power is distributed more evenly. A plurality of viewpoints is appreciated and differences are celebrated'.[30] If the post-modernist understanding of community becomes fully embedded in contemporary culture, the issue will not be whether one is in or out of community; rather, it will be a matter of which community one chooses to belong to. According to Leuze, 'communities which are open to diversity and hold a dynamic view of knowledge and language will be more conducive to post-modern perspectives,' whereas 'communities which seek to be homogenous, which maintain a static understanding of knowledge and a literalist interpretation of language will be closed to the diversity which is inherent in post-modern thought'.[31] While the latter perspective may be consciously employed in order to halt the advance of post-modern thought, this may have an adverse effect on a community, since changing perspectives are inevitable. History appears to teach this lesson in the case of the Catholic Church.

A challenge facing religious institutions at the beginning of a new millennium is whether they can critically embrace the post-modernist perspective and its attending culture of post-modernity; whether they can embrace unity-in-diversity, allowing all viewpoints to be accorded value, while at the same time preserving the essential parameters of belief, structure and practice.

Globalisation

The most recent term used to name the cultural reality of our day among religious educators is that of globalisation. This reflects the use of this as a key term among economists, social scientists and politicians, who believe that we have entered the age of supranational and global unification. Friedrich Schweitzer argues that the concept of globalisation should replace earlier interpretations of the contemporary cultural reality. In his view, 'we should now speak of globalisation or of the "global age" rather than of modernisation or post-modernity'[32] and religious educators should adopt this key perspective offered by social scientists for the human journey into the third millennium. He cites many authors who go beyond the popular understanding of globalisation as that of a worldwide open market and just another step within the development of capitalist economy. In their understanding, the concept of globalisation includes a cultural process that may deeply change people's lives, 'and it must be considered a social force that may influence our religious beliefs and deepest loyalties'.[33] Consequently, the dawning 'global age' is a fundamental challenge for religious education.

I disagree with Schweitzer's position in regard to replacing the concept of post-modernity with that of globalisation, not least because one loses the philosophical dimension inherent in post-modernism, which is essential for a comprehensive understanding of our contemporary culture. I would rather view globalisation as a central element in post-modernity. With that in mind, I offer some thoughts regarding the effects of the globalisation element of post-modernity on religious values and its challenge to religious education.

It is possible to isolate three key elements in the challenge of globalisation to religious education. The first and main effect of the 'global age' is that it brings about a thorough relativisation of religion. Peter Beyer points out that when cultures are brought closer together the worldviews or grand narratives that could formerly be taken for granted 'appear to be to a significant extent arbitrary'.[34] The celebration of diversity that is characteristic of post-modern thinking is seen more sharply on a global level and the issue of religious truth becomes an increasingly subjective matter.

A second effect of globalisation results in the privatisation of religion. Schweitzer remarks that 'if everyday life functions without religious authority and without existential questions, such authority and such questions become more and more removed from public life'.[35] If they do have a place it is only in the private sphere.

Fundamentalism is now regarded as a third effect of globalisation. This is really counter-globalisation as it attempts to confront the 'global age' by upholding traditional authority. Fundamentalism is often regarded as a psychological aberration, but it may also stem from the fear of losing one's personal or religious identity.

The Opportunities and Challenges of a Post-Modern Millennium

While globalisation encompasses a significant dimension of post-modernity and requires close scrutiny, I will now turn to the broader dimensions of our contemporary cultural reality. David Tracy points out that the challenge of post-modernity to Christian faith differs from that of modernity. He views post-modernity as a new sensibility, which is more open to Christian faith than modernity.[36] Many commentators agree with this position, while others believe that contemporary culture is undermining not only Church-related faith, but also the requisite openness that is necessary for believing. I would rather view contemporary culture from the perspective of David Tracy, particularly because of its new openness to the mystical, the spiritual and to new forms of interactive community.

New Openness to the Spiritual

It is my experience that while the majority of young people either reject, or are indifferent to, institutionalised religion they are very open to the religious or spiritual dimension of life. The most recent statistics show that the vast majority of young

ng is conceived. As
moved away from
non-flexible, rigid
in God is still very
d is that of a very
around us, a life-
ity and that God is
an life, animal and
untains – God is in
nce to two surveys
h demonstrated a
nal God and a fifty
per cent increase in belief in God as 'some sort of Spirit' or 'Life-Force', Joseph Dunne remarked that 'there certainly seems to be a marked shift in the nature of what counts as "religion" – a shift away from faith in a historically specific revelation, articulated theologically in doctrines such as the Trinity and the Incarnation, towards a more diffuse form of what might be called spirituality'.[38]

Many young people today are searching for what they name as experiential religious encounters which, in their experience, the traditional religious institutions are unable to provide. Some of them even want to recover a Jesus who is 'real' and connected to them rather than to the highly suspect religious body. Tom Beaudoin believes that as well as living religiously in and through popular culture, the rising generation in North America has taken religion into its own hands in two specific ways. 'First', he says, 'they have a widespread regard for paganism – however vaguely defined'.[39] This is evidenced in popular books and record store offerings as well as in the profusion of internet information on paganism. The second way in which young people personalise or de-institutionalise religion, according to Beaudoin, is 'through a growing enchantment with mysticism'.[40] Again, this can be witnessed in book shops, music stores and in popular discussion. 'As practiced by [young people]', he says, 'mysticism is defined as broadly as paganism and is often expressed as religious eclecticism. [Young people] take symbols, values and rituals from various religious traditions and combine them into their personal spirituality'.[41]

The results of an in-depth interview process among Irish youth revealed similar characteristics. These young people, like their North American counterparts, prized diversity and tolerance for various points of view and ways of life, saying that 'there is not any one particular set of beliefs that fits who you are'.[42] One had joined a 'rainbow church'. Others appreciated a plurality of viewpoints and celebrated differences. 'Many elements of Buddhism as well as many of those in the Christian tradition' were also valued.[43]

The appeal of mysticism to the rising generation may well be a symptom of a strong reaction against the rationality of modernity and not just a fanciful flight from traditional (inherited) religious practice. David Tracy argues that delving into the mystical dimension of life is a way of being prophetic, reacting against the 'drive to sameness, the modern western scientific, technological, culture'.[44] Beaudoin expresses a similar view when he points out that the youth of today 'may feel that our culture's untrammelled trust in reason is not enough, that grand narratives (about power or patriarchy) swallow our individuality...'.[45] Challenging the modern world in this way places today's youth in a post-modern context. Tracy suggests that 'the recovery of mystical readings of the prophetic core of Judaism and Christianity is one of the surest signs of a post modern sensibility'.[46]

The renewed openness to the spiritual dimension of life among the rising generation, in whatever form it takes, provides an opportunity for religious educators to build on an existing foundation. Indeed, the penchant for the spiritual which is evident today does not always find expression in pagan forms; very often it is Christian or Jewish at its core, as those *[handwritten margin notes:]* careful as dont want to compare and make Christianity superior

[handwritten margin notes:] new curriculum is pushing them away too

...test. Michael Paul ...ituality can be born ...onship of faith, the ...phetic challenges to ...nversation about the ...earch for wholeness ... is evident among ...n, is at least open to, ...he Christian story in ...expression.

...ligion

One of the themes that characterises the spirituality of post-modern youth is that organised religion and other institutions are suspect. In this context, it is important to point out that the apathy towards inherited religious institutions reflects an indifference towards institutions in general, this being a hallmark of post-modernity. In other words, institutional religious faith is a victim of a post-modern culture.

The Catholic theologian, Robert Ludwig, while acknowledging that new spiritual opportunities are emerging as young people 'become more and more open to the experiences that lie at the core of [Catholic] tradition', points out that the new generation is 'increasingly alienated from the institutional Church'.[48] The analysis of in-depth interviews with young people certainly reveals a de-emphasis on, and in some cases a rejection of, organised religion. One young Irish woman had this to say: 'Right now I would see myself as having a loose affiliation with the Catholic Church... I have my own beliefs and my own faith and I am quite happy with that'.[49] A young man from a socially deprived area commented: 'The Church as an institution is very middle class and therefore excludes people of my class. The young people with whom I work, the so-called underclass, all feel alienated from the Church and not only from the Church, but from all institutions of the State'.[50] After interviewing young people from all over the United States, Cohen discovered some diversity in religious attitudes, but a response typical of many young people was expressed in the words of one respondent who explained that 'one of the reasons I don't go to Church like I should [is that] they're just hypocrites'.[51] Beaudoin concurs in saying that this is the most common charge that he has heard from young people about religion. 'The perception of hypocrisy', he says, 'is one reason religion is not a security blanket but a wet blanket to so many'.[52] Howe and Strauss report that 'religion ranks behind friends, home, school, music and television as factors [young people] believe are having the greatest influence on their generation'.[53] However, when one looks at the broader picture in the results of Cohen's research across the United States, it is clear that more than criticism is afoot. In the book, *Twentysomething American Dream*, one of those interviewed, Lavona, expresses another common attitude among young people: 'What the hell's going to church for? These days you've got to take religion in your own hands'.[54]

New Openness to Community

One feature of the philosophy of post-modernism that appears to augur well for a community-based religious faith such as our own is the new non-individualistic attitude that is replacing the individualism of modernism. As one young person put it: 'Many young people today are moving away from the individualism that was characteristic of the era that we seem to be leaving behind, the kind of individualism you see in modern Irish society...'.[55]

This renewed sense of the importance of community does not deny the significance of the individual; rather, the conception is that the individual cannot be understood apart from his or her role in the community. From the post-modern perspective communities that are open to diversity will be more attractive to the post-modern sensibility, whereas

Fail to consider the kids is problematic (handwritten annotation)

is (where we all
e themselves off
ne post-modern

lern culture with
experience is of
When it comes to
now best to live,
or. As one young
by paying really
close attention to everything that I do, and I ascertain what is important by looking at how things feel inside, by reflecting on how something affects me spiritually and emotionally'.[56] She goes on to say: 'I believe there is no absolute right or wrong, apart from, perhaps, hurting a child'.[57] Another young person had this to say: 'I do not think that there are any absolute truths, any absolute right or wrong. It depends on each person – whatever is true for them'.[58]

Culture: The Key Issue

The analysis of my empirical research supports the view widely held in the literature on cultural influence, namely, the manner in which people experience reality, especially the young, is culture-bound, and their ideas, values and general attitudes to life are largely determined by the type of culture to which they are exposed. Metaphorically speaking, culture is a matter of life or death, and sometimes literally so. Thus any educational or religious educational endeavour that does not take account of the contemporary cultural milieu in which all age groups, especially the young, are immersed is destined to be less than adequate. In this regard, it is important for the adult members of a faith community, especially those who are 'official' teachers, to remember that their ideas, values and attitudes are culture-bound too, even if from a different cultural experience. This recognition will encourage intercultural dialogue between student and teacher.

The relationship between religious nurture and religious education needs to be reconsidered. In a sense, there is no more room for simple nurture in religion. This points to the vital importance of the questions raised and views expressed by the authors of the following chapters. If religious education is going to play its indispensable role in future right relations within nations and among the nations of the world, the nature, purpose and aim of religious education needs to be carefully explored.

Notes

1. O. Brennan, *Cultures Apart?* (Dublin: Veritas Publications, 2001), p. 13.
2. E. Doyle McCarthy, *Knowledge as Culture: The New Sociology of Knowledge* (London: Routledge, 1996), p. 5.
3. T. H. Groome, *Christian Religious Education: Sharing our Story and Vision* (San Francisco: Harper and Row, 1980).
4. M. Warren, *Communications and Cultural Analysis* (Westport CT: Bergin and Garvey, 1992) p. 6.
5. T. Beaudoin, *Virtual Faith: The Irreverent Spiritual Quest of Generation X* (Jossey-Bass, San Francisco, 1998) p. 22.
6. M. P. Gallagher, *Clashing Symbols: An Introduction to Faith and Culture* (London: Darton, Longman & Todd, 1997) p. 13.
7. C. Geertz, *The Interpretation of Cultures* (New York: Basic Books, 1973) p. 89.
8. A. Shorter, *Towards a Theology of Inculturation* (New York: Orbis Books, 1988) p. 5
9. L. Kroeber and D. Kluckhohn, *Culture, A Critical Review of Concepts and Definitions* (New York: Vintage Books, 1983).
10. Shorter, op.cit., p. 20.
11. *Irish Times* 8 January 2003.
12. Brennan, op.cit., p. 29.
13. C. Taylor, *The Ethics of Authenticity* (Cambridge, MA: Harvard University Press, 1991).

14. Ibid, p. 120.
15. T. E. Leuze, *Is Shared Christian Praxis Postmodern? An Anglo-American Postmodern Consideration*. Paper presented at the APRRE Annual Meeting (Orlando, Florida, 1998).
16. N. Murphy, *Theology in the Age of Scientific Reasoning*, Cornell Studies in the Philosophy of Religion (Ithaca, NY: Cornell University Press, 1990) p. 201.
17. Gill, *Learning to Learn: Towards a Philosophy of Education* (Atlantic Highlands, NJ, Humanities Press International, 1993) p. 48.
18. M. Sorri and J. H. Gill, *A Postmodern Epistemology: Language, Truth and Body* (Lewiston, NY: Edwin Mellin Press, 1989) p. 1.
19. Gill, op.cit., p. 48.
20. Leuze, op.cit., p. 151.
21. Ibid.
22. S. Aronowitz and H. A. Giroux, *Postmodern Education: Politics, Culture and Social Criticism* (Minneapolis: University of Minnesota Press, 1991) pp. 188-189.
23. L. Vygotsky, *Mind in Society: The Development of Higher Psychological Processes*, ed. M. Cole et al; (Cambridge MA: Harvard University Press, 1978) pp. 88-90.
24. Leuze, op.cit., p. 147.
25. Murphy, op.cit.
26. Ibid.
27. U. Bronfenbrenner, *The Ecology of Human Development: Experiments by Nature and Design* (Cambridge MA: Harvard University Press, 1979).
28. Leuze, op.cit.
29. Taylor, op.cit., p. 58.
30. Leuze, op.cit., p. 155.
31. Ibid., p. 154.
32. F. Schweitzer, *The Fourth R for the Third Millenium*, ed. Leslie J. Francis, Jeff Astley, Mandy Robbins (Dublin: Lindisfarne Books, 2001) p. 159.
33. Ibid., p. 160.
34. P. Beyer, *Religion and Globalisation* (London: Sage, 1994) p. 2.
35. Schweitzer, op.cit., p. 163.
36. D. Tracy, *Theology and the Many Faces of Postmodernity*, Theology Today 51, (1994) pp. 104-114.
37. Brennan, ibid., p. 16.
38. J. Dunne, 'Religion and Modernity: Reading the Signs', in *Faith and Culture in the Irish Context*, ed E. G. Cassidy (Dublin: Veritas Publications, 1996) p. 53.

39. Beaudoin, *Virtual Faith*, p. 25.
40. Ibid., p. 25.
41. Ibid., p. 25.
42. Brennan, op.cit., p. 163.
43. Ibid.
44. Tracy, op.cit.
45. Beaudoin, op.cit., p. 26.
46. Tracy, op.cit., p. 114.
47. Gallagher, op.cit., p. 52.
48. R. Ludwig, *Reconstructing Catholicism: for a New Generation*, (NY: Crossroad, 1995) p. 9.
49. Brennan, op.cit., p. 22.
50. Ibid., p. 37.
51. M. L. Cohen, *The Twentysomething American Dream: A Cross-Country Quest for a Generation*, (NY: Dutton, 1993) p. 97.
52. Beaudoin, op.cit., p. 25.
53. N. Howe and B. Strauss, *Thirteenth Gen : Abort, Retry, Ignore, Fail?* (NY: Vintage Books, 1993) p. 187.
54. Cohen, op.cit., p. 183.
55. Brennan, op.cit., p. 16.
56. Ibid., p. 15.
57. Ibid., p. 15.
58. Ibid., p. 23.

Religious

It is my conviction that religious education is one of the most crucial issues needing to be addressed in Ireland today. It is also my belief that religious education is considered by many people to be unimportant to our country as a whole and that it does not achieve supreme acknowledgment in the Christian churches nor in society. This is partly due to the narrow understanding of the meaning and purpose of religious education. If religious education is perceived to be concerned about proselytising and indoctrination, then society is right in regarding this activity as insignificant. However, if educating religiously is understood as that which pertains to the centre of human life and contributes to the quality of our being in the world, then religious education is an indispensable endeavour. With that in mind, this chapter attempts to set an overall framework for religious education in contemporary Ireland. In doing this, I rely heavily on the seminal thinking of Gabriel Moran.

The Current Reality of Religious Education

Religious education in Ireland is narrowly understood as that which takes place within the school setting. Predominantly directed at people between the ages of five and eighteen,

like england its not
taken seriously either
no universal definition
making it worse

the title varying from
knowledge', to 'religious
) 'religious education',
the school. In Roman
nger children concerns
d doctrines of their faith
:he sacraments of first
Confirmation. This is
curriculum content for
s a deeper exploration of
arlier in life. Religious
iic subject at all levels of
the post-primary school and students have the option of taking
this subject for State examination.

This story of Irish religious education points to a number
of problems inherent in its implementation. The first
concerns the absence of a discipline that can be accurately
named religious education. With little or no recognition of
the adult population, religious education is addressed almost
exclusively to school-aged children and even at that, is
considered to be an appendage to *real* education. Not
considered to be of primary importance, some schools
allocate a minimum of resources to religious education and
people, for the most part, remain unconcerned.

A major problem inherent in Irish religious education pertains
to the babel of languages used to describe what takes place.
Although they possess varying meanings and differing sets of
assumptions, the words catechetics, religion, religious
knowledge, religious studies, religious instruction, Christian
Doctrine, Christian education and religious education are judged
to be synonymous and are used interchangeably. As a result,
different people mean different things when using the term
'religious education'. Attaining consensus regarding the use of
terms is a necessary and essential prerequisite for any discipline or
field of study, particularly that of religious education.

This babel of languages and interchangeability of terms has led to confusion of purpose and a crisis of identity regarding the activity of religious education and the role of religious educators. Thus, the third problem Ireland needs to address concerns the purpose of religious education. What is the purpose of religious education? The variety of interpretations has resulted in a multiplicity of understandings of the purpose or aim of religious education. This situation points to a fourth concern, namely, the absence of a coherent theory of religious education, a theory that would outline the philosophy, assumptions, and foundational principles and, at the same time, serve to dissipate the confusion of purpose and identity that abounds.

The story of Irish religious education related above points to the reality of the discipline in many areas of the world, as many well-renowned international religious educators will attest. Religious educators such as Gabriel Moran and Kieran Scott, for instance, continually seek to address these issues and contribute to their clarification. For over thirty years, Gabriel Moran has noted the absence of a field of religious education, has sought to break open the meaning of words in order to bring about linguistic clarity, and has called for an adequate theory of the subject.[1] Kieran Scott acknowledges similar concerns.[2] Calling for order in the area of religious education, Scott contends that the field is not clearly defined. No consensus has been reached with regard to key terms. The purpose of religious education is unclear and more attention must be given to its theory.

The purpose of this chapter is to explore the four above-mentioned problems in an effort to uncover and unveil a fuller meaning of religious education. Our task now is to bring order to the chaos. How can we resolve this identity crisis? Where do we go from here? We are faced with a choice. We can remain as we are or we can shift our focus. We need a new theory, a new philosophy of education.

In keeping with the thought of Moran, I would like to suggest a way forward by shifting the fundamental framework in which we see the field. My suggestion is that we turn to education generally as the overall framework for religious education.[3]

Education as the Overall Framework for Religious Education

In moving to education as the overall framework for religious education, it is necessary to exercise a word of caution. If education is to be properly understood, it is essential to distinguish between education and school. While almost all writers on education would agree that the words 'education' and 'school' are not synonymous, in practice these terms are frequently used interchangeably, with the assumption that education is owned by the school. Such an assumption places an unwarranted burden on the school, as well as serving to exclude other forms of education. It is vital to acknowledge that schooling, while it is extremely important, is only one form of education, and that several non-schooling forms of education are in existence. We need to name, include and develop these forms of education in fostering an intelligent religious life. It is essential, therefore, that a definition of religious education would include such factors as family life, prayer, and social action.

The shift to an educational model as the basis for understanding religious education necessitates an attempt to create a new field of religious education for which there is, as yet, no adequate language. In his attempt to wrestle with this issue, Gabriel Moran began by exploring and critiquing the ecclesiastical language used to describe and control the meaning of religious education. This first language comprised the two components of theology and catechetics/Christian education. The result was that religious education was reduced to the language of the Church. It was equated with catechetics in the Catholic tradition and with Christian education in Protestant circles. Catechetics and Christian education became a kind of practical theology. Believing that the term *religious* education has a broader meaning than either catechetics or Christian education, Moran stated that any attempt to break open the language barrier of the Church must contrast two meanings of the term, one whose roots are deeply embedded in Christianity, the other whose meaning is deeper and broader:

- Officials of a Church indoctrinate children to obey an official Church.
- The whole religious community educates the whole religious community to make free and intelligent religious decisions vis-à-vis the whole world.[4]

The existence of these two definitions points to the confusion concerning the meaning and understanding of religious education. What appears to be happening is that 'people are using the same words but in different semantic universes.'[5]

In striving to distinguish between these two meanings of religious education, it is important to note that the first meaning contains an inner consistency comprising agent, action, recipient and desired result. Being clearly identified with catechesis in the Roman Catholic tradition and with Christian Education in the Protestant tradition, this first meaning provides too narrow a framework in which to work. My preference lies with the second interpretation, which recognises and acknowledges the community as being both the agent and recipient of education, with education taking place within the total life of the body. Mutuality becomes the hallmark of education and this is no longer understood as that which happens to children of a certain age within a school setting. Rather, education applies to each individual throughout his or her life.

In practice, this understanding varies in accordance with a person's stage of development. Human experience becomes the connecting link between all stages of growth, with the individual continually adapting and realigning oneself with the environment. Religious education is community based and is understood and lived from the position of adulthood as psychological, social and religious maturity.

This understanding and practice from the stance of adulthood is illustrative of the fact that school has never been a good setting for religious education. While the school does contribute to the formation of an intellectually religious person, religious attitudes and values are primarily learned in the community. The function of the religious community is to demonstrate a life into which the child can grow. In this respect, it can be seen that religious education, as it matures towards adulthood, brings together the best of education and the best of religion; it is that which takes place at the intersection of religion and education.

The Intersection of Religion and Education

The shift to an educational framework, as the basis for understanding religious education, necessitates an attempt to create a new field for which there is, as yet, no adequate language. Gabriel Moran talks about religious education being found at the intersection of religion and education. He states that religious education is the obvious term to denote this meeting. What is truly envisaged in the intersection of religion and education is a religious education that (a) from the educational stance would challenge the quality and purpose of all education and (b) from the religious angle would examine educational practices in existing religious institutions. In other words, education and religion need one another. Education needs the challenge of religion in order not to close in on itself and religion needs education so that the Christian Churches preserve within themselves some of the elements of a religious education.

ld, necessarily, bring
ge the adequacy of
s, as well as the semi-
ach a position reflects
sing the plurality of
s a tolerable level of
one recognises the
There is a new
into an educational
f religion (ignorance,
diminished and, at the
to be central to life,
central to the way we live. Religion needs to be central to family life, work life and leisure life. Indeed, coming from the Latin *religio*, the word *religion* means tying together, knitting together, that is, bringing together all the different facets of our lives.

Towards a Fuller Meaning of Religious Education

In advocating a new meaning of religious education it is necessary to step back from that question to examine the term itself. In this regard, we have to distinguish between the actual meaning of religious education that is in existence and an advocative meaning, that is, what the term should mean. In advocating a particular meaning of a term, one does not begin from neutral ground. Rather, one begins by trying to discover or recover a realm of meaning that is, in some sense, latent in the operative meaning, but has been obscured by the dominant meaning. While it is possible to argue that anything can be meant by a particular word or term, an advocative definition, if it is to be authentic, necessitates etymological and historical knowledge. It also requires concrete examples to exemplify the advocated meaning.

The discussion of the distinction between a descriptive and an advocative definition helps to situate the question

[Handwritten margin note: Does not consider that religion is decreasing need to be able to be critical if want to teach younger generations]

regarding the meaning of the term religious education. Currently there are two competing meanings for how religious education functions in contemporary language. One understanding can be traced back to the liberal theology that was dominant at the beginning of the twentieth century. This is reflected in John Dewey's use of the term 'operative' in his keynote speech at the inauguration of the Religious Education Association. In this context, the term religious education has a very broad meaning. The second strand of the current meaning of religious education is designated 'Christian education' in Protestantism and 'catechetics' in Roman Catholicism, both of which are associated with producing practising Church members. For an advocative meaning of the term, religious education has to include not only a religious institutional enterprise, but also whole areas that are not currently under any religious organisation. Indeed, the modern understanding of religious education functions neither as part of education nor as part of religion. Therefore, it is neither very religious nor very educational. Unless this linguistic pattern is broken, theorising about religious education is likely to reinforce the currently inadequate pattern of institutionalisation.

In his attempt to conceptualise an advocated meaning of religious education, Moran posits two settings – 'school' and 'laboratory' – the latter connoting family, work and leisure.[6] While not equating education and school, he argues that the churches need good schools where religion can be taught and studied. Two distinct religious orientations exist within the school setting. One concerns the study of religion from the perspective of a specific tradition, while the other involves a certain distinction from one's tradition and the study of religion in an intersubjective manner. The latter approach, on its own, is inadequate, but combined with the first is a crucial component of religious education.

Within the laboratory setting, there are three main orientations to learning: the family/community, the work site, and the 'retreat'. In each of these settings the religious question can organically emerge. Coe, for example, pointed to the 'measureless potential of the family as an agency of Christian education'.[7] While Moran agrees that the family is an essential element, he also states that it is very important not to romanticise it. C. Ellis Nelson also shares this view. Acknowledging the family as a very important agent in communicating Christian faith, he believes that a system of Christian nurture cannot be based on the family alone 'because the family is more an agent of culture and society than it is an independent unit'.[8] The family, therefore, needs to be provided with communal settings if it is to be effective in its task. There is need for learning within families, learning between children and adults of all ages, learning between the very old and the very young, learning between families and all social institutions.

As can be seen, therefore, education and religion need one another. For an advocative meaning of the term, religious education has to include not only Church-sponsored activities, but also the teaching of religion as a curriculum subject, that is, things that have purposes of formation, but also non-purposes of formation. In talking about religious education, we need to include the key forms of life that touch people's lives: family, schooling, the workplace and leisure time.

In distinguishing among these sets of terms, Moran's overriding intention is to promote a theory that cannot be reduced to the language of the Church. Religion and education need to be consistent and complementary partners. Religion's role is to challenge education and enable it to rediscover the richness of what it is to be religious. Conversely, the scene is changed when the affairs of religion are brought into the educational framework – the true essence of education is revealed.

It is now possible to establish some precepts necessary for a field of religious education:

- Rather than comprising abstract or diluted generalities, the religious aspect of religious education must be concrete, distinctive, and unparalleled. Such a maxim can be provided by an educational setting in which religious doctrines are reconstructed with reverence, intelligence, and patience.
- The establishment of a grand synthesis is not the aim of religious education. Rather, it seeks to foster greater appreciation and understanding of one's own religious life as well as that of other people.
- A third axiom is the provision of a place in which the past can be handed on in the form of ritual and historical study. In this regard, it is important to note that, while the teaching of religion in the school environment offers an invaluable contribution to religious education, it is inadequate in its ability to sustain a religious life. In sum, the encounter between religion and education is likely to result in two things: (1) a transformation of the new religious group from within, resulting in changed institutions and in new methods for transmitting the religious life to the next generation; (2) a conversation with other religious groups that will eventually lead to increased tolerance and mutual understanding.[9]

Towards a Wider Conversation

The current position is that religious education occurs between a constricted, prevailing meaning and a potential meaning too broad to be understood. Moran acknowledges that it is possible to explore it from two angles – by *describing* the term religious education and by *exploring* its meaning.[10] What he has done, in the course of his writings, is to unveil the potential meaning in an effort to depict what could be included in the term. The pertinent question is *meaning*

[Handwritten annotation:] Don't like Morans passionate involvement and understanding as it elevates Christianity above others
good way to describe working in a Catholic School

...ant changes in the ...stating questions, ...deeper levels of ... is that words are ...n that necessitates ... if the full meaning ...n is to emerge. ...ent of religious ...individual learning ...nclude a better ... well as increased ...very language are elements that can be called 'religious', manifested through expressions concerned with the ultimate in life. For example, a Christian, Jew, and Muslim assimilate different religious ideas because of the language to which they are exposed and nurtured. Religious education begins to emerge with the comparison of different religious languages. In this respect, religious education can be understood as the attempt to gather many religious languages into a single conversation. In Moran's words, the invitation is 'to hold, in fruitful tension, a passionate involvement in one religious group and a sympathetic understanding of other religious groups'.[12] Such an endeavour is crucial for the development and spread of understanding, tolerance, and peace in the world.

Moran's attempt to establish a cohesive meaning of religious education has led him to call for a wider conversation, one that is international, interreligious, intergenerational, and interinstitutional. Religious education, he notes, is concerned with the 'religious life of the human race and with bringing people within the influence of that life'.[13] In Moran's conceptualisation, religious education has a dual nature: understanding religion, and formation in being religious. It is akin to Parker J. Palmer's vocation and avocation.

My vocation is the spiritual life, the quest for God, which relies on the eye of the heart. My avocation is education, the quest for knowledge, which relies on the eye of the mind.[14]

These two natures of religious education are related, but must be clearly distinguished.

Two Aims of Religious Education

The two aims of religious education are related, distinct, and of equal importance. Religious education here comprises two forms, two processes, and two aims, all of which take place within a multitude of settings. Both activities are described as 'teaching people'.[15] This does not mean that the person doing the teaching is a person with the title 'teacher'. Rather, the ultimate source of the teaching is the human community and the non-human environment.

A second noteworthy aspect in the distinction between the two aims concerns the difference between the noun 'religion' and the adjective 'religious'. The modern use of the word religion is ambiguous in that it can be used to refer to a subject on the school curriculum or it may allude to a set of practices carried out by a particular religious group. The adjective religious, on the other hand, reveals the particular way in which one can be religious. This ambiguity concerning religion is advantageous to the extent that it points to the inner connection between 'teaching people to be religious in a particular way' and 'teaching people religion'.[16] These aims are not simply parallel processes in which disparate groups engage. Rather, one or other process can predominate in the life of an individual at any particular moment.

A Word on Teaching

In discussing the aims of religious education, the question of perspective is pivotal. The use of the verb 'to teach' in both

need to consider religion isn't influencing in the same way

ns of teaching are ng involves showing succinctly, it means ntually includes how ling stands in stark prevalent in today's explanations. While ry important, other d.

aching the Way

gious socialisation as articulated by Ellis Nelson,[17] Westerhoff,[18] Westerhoff and Kennedy Neville,[19] and Marthaler.[20] It concerns the initiation, formation and socialisation of each new generation who will carry out the practices, ritual, and mission of the religious group. This work of forming people into being religious and behaving in a religious manner is carried on by the adult members of the community. The religious community, however, needs a boundary in order to provide intimacy, support, and identity for its members.

The importance of socialisation is highlighted by the emphasis Ellis Nelson places on the manner in which culture/religion influences a person's life.[21] A child is surrounded by religion from the moment of birth. Indeed, religion shapes a person's selfhood long before he or she becomes self-consciously aware. 'What is unknown,' he writes, 'is that culture is internalised in persons and institutionalised in society. Culture is the meaning of life that is transmitted to others, especially children'.[22] The world-view of a particular way of being religious is mediated directly to children by those who nurture and socialise them and becomes an integral part of their self-understanding. 'Imitation is the method by which a person appropriates the style of life of the group in which he comes to selfhood'.[23] The values imbibed by young children, therefore, are, to a large extent, an extension of the values of the nurturing group. In this regard, Ellis Nelson writes:

> The child does not come into self-awareness and then discover culture; he finds and defines himself in a particular culture... the appropriation of his parents' way of seeing and living is built deep into his personality – partly consciously – and it permeates his whole being.[24]

The symbols that give meaning and explanations of life, therefore, play a very important role in the transmission of a religious way of life to each individual.

John H. Westerhoff,[25] and Westerhoff and Kennedy Neville,[26] advocate a process of intentional religious socialisation. By religious socialisation, they mean 'a process consisting of lifelong formal and informal mechanisms, through which persons sustain and transmit their faith (world view, value system) and life style'.[27] While they acknowledge the major influence of family and peers, their primary interest in calling for *intentional religious socialisation* lies in the socialisation that takes place in faith communities. Without a community of faith supporting and transmitting the family's Christian vision, the task facing religious socialisation is very difficult. They believe that 'an intentional community of faith remains the essential key to religious socialisation'.[28] The great challenge, therefore, is to enable local churches to become religious communities in which the Christian faith can be imbibed.

Berard L. Marthaler enters the conversation by distinguishing between faith and belief. Faith is a personal response to gift whose meaning is mediated by specific beliefs.[29] The socialisation, therefore, of a person into a particular religious tradition is more concerned with beliefs than faith. In this regard, he is in agreement with Westerhoff that 'faith cannot be taught by any method of instruction and that religions can only be caught'.[30] The seeds of faith can be awakened, nourished, and developed by catechesis or education in faith. The role of catechesis is to unearth the mysteries lying beneath the surface of everyday life, as well as to recount the story and transmit the wisdom of a particular tradition. In this regard, he names three objectives of the socialisation model of religious education: growth in person faith, religious affiliation, and the maintenance and transmission of a religious tradition.

In teaching to be religious, the aim is to teach people to be religious in a particular way, that is, in the way of Judaism, Catholicism, or Islam. The object here is singular – 'the practice of one concrete set of activities that exclude other ways of acting,' with the teacher comprising the community and the environment.[31] Although the parish is deemed to be the place where people are taught to be religious in a Catholic way, it is the liturgical community that forms the heart of this teaching. In this setting, energies for social justice flow from common worship and individual prayer. 'The experience of prayer and the overflow into moral engagement with today's world,' Moran notes, 'is what forms the person as Christian'.[32] It is, to use an ecclesiastical term, the way in which diakonia is manifested in parish life (that is, preaching by service resulting in works of justice).

Westerhoff and Kennedy Neville strongly emphasise the role of the Christian community in transmitting its vision and way of life to young people, an emphasis receiving increasing attention today.[33] Their contention is that religious education must be 'centered on the life and work of the community of faith'.[34] People are socialised, they continue, 'by the space and ecology in which they live'.[35] The local Church community offers an endless hidden curriculum to all members, one that is a powerful teaching force. In this regard, Westerhoff and Kennedy Neville call for the life and structures of the faith community to be renewed and suggests that it begins with the adult members of the community. Not detracting from the primordial role of the family as the first and powerful agency of socialisation, they, like Moran, note that their efforts will be ineffective without the support of a vibrant faith community. Furthermore, people require the experience of being part of a group that celebrates the presence and action of God in a sacramental fashion.

The first aim of religious education begins at birth. From the first moments of life, a child is taught by an adult community to be religious. Through persistent learning, continued demonstrations of care and compassion and ongoing celebrations of a living liturgy, the adult community provides the young with what they most need. Indeed, liturgical worship is the predominant form of teaching in the religious community.

Teaching the way means showing people how to live and how to die through the embodiment of a set of beliefs, symbols, and actions. All of these link people to the abiding religious questions like, 'Where do I come from?', 'Where am I going?', and 'Why?' In this regard, Maria Harris describes one way: catechesis, whose narrative centre is found in Acts 2: 22-24, 32.[36] Westerhoff and Kennedy Neville are in agreement.[37] In their view, Christian catechesis is to educate members of the Church to take responsibility for continuing the mission of Jesus Christ in the world today. Moran would surely concur.

Second Aim: Teaching to Understand Religion

The second aim of religious education is mostly a matter of the mind and involves the provision of an understanding of religion, including one's own religion. An openness to understand is an antidote to the tendency to attack, belittle, condemn, or dismiss what may, on the surface, seem bizarre or absurd. The test of genuine understanding will be gauged by whether or not one is ready to listen attentively, reflect calmly, and judge fairly.

The second aim of religious education is to teach people to understand religion. In this process the aim is 'to understand.' This activity, according to Moran necessitates a double conversation: 'the dialogue between religions and the dialogue of religion(s) with secular life'.[38] While such an understanding of religion can take place anywhere, the classroom has been intentionally established as the ideal setting for this process. The teaching of religion in the school context is an essential component of the field of religious education. Mindful of the fact that teaching involves showing someone how to do something, the responsibility for showing someone how to employ words and concepts in order to understand religion falls on the school. In this situation, the student is enabled to ascertain a deeper level of inquiry than would be available outside the classroom. Moran argues for the inclusion of religion in the school setting, and states that 'school is precisely where religion belongs'.[39] Religion is an academic category. More precisely, it is 'an idea and a method posited by scholars,' indicating the intention to exercise the mind in comprehending not only one's own religious tradition, but also that of other people.[40]

Westerhoff clearly differs from Moran's position when he questions the undergirding paradigm of the Church's educational ministry (the schooling-instructional model).[41] Perceiving religious education as nurturing a person in faith in the presence of a worshipping, witnessing community, his belief is that the school-instructional paradigm undermines any process of religious socialisation in the minds of catechists and members of the parish community. The Churches, in his opinion, should avoid modelling their educational methodology and approaches on the promulgations of secular education. But this is not Moran's intention here.

Moran's reflection on how to teach religion leads him to postulate what it means 'to show a person how to use words and concepts so as to understand a field called religion'.[42] His response to this question is fourfold:

1. The teacher must intelligibly present the available material.
2. The teacher must enable the religious text to act as mediator between the community of another era and the community of today.
3. In order to facilitate the understanding of religious meaning, the teacher must participate in the meaning to a certain degree. In other words, the teacher must step into the shoes of the writer and perceive the world from that perspective.
4. The teacher draws upon the experience of students and teachers.

Unfortunately, in the United States, the task of teaching people to understand religion has been relegated, almost entirely, to religious institutions, a burden that is too heavy to carry. The parish is not well designed for this task. Rather, its assignment is to teach people to be religious in a Catholic way. In the Republic of Ireland, for example, the situation is reversed, with the full chore of teaching religion being the sole task of the school.

While the word 'religion' in the second aim is written in the singular, its object is plural. It begins from the perspective of one's own religion, but entails comparisons with other religions, a factor that leads to a better understanding of one's own religion.

Comparing and Contrasting the Two Aims

A complete contrast between the two faces of religious education would involve describing the who, what, how, where, and why of this enterprise. Indeed, the recipients of religious education will vary according to each face of religious education. In the first type, the recipients are inquirers of a religious community. Here the focus is very particular: This group of people either desire to be, or are socialised into, the way of life and ritual practice of the faith community. In this regard, most religious bodies, such as the Christian, Jewish, and Muslim faiths, concentrate on children. By adopting the premises of modern education, many religious groups understand religious education as an activity that begins at the age of four or five, thereby neglecting the most formative time in children's lives. Moran is a strong advocate of lifelong education, but he says that, 'an education that deserves the name 'lifelong' would necessarily start at birth, at the latest, and continue until death'.[43] If one follows this path, it implies that the religious body shows special concern for the parents of young children.

In the second face of religious education, understanding religion, the recipients span all generations, from young child to older adult, taking account of the fact that the capacity to understand religion develops gradually over many years. The ability to exercise critical judgments about one's own religion in relation to the religion of others demands a certain maturity. In this regard, Moran believes that 'the concentration of so much religious education in the years of elementary school lacks any clear logic'.[44] Furthermore, since some basis of comparison is necessary to understand any phenomenon, a manageable diversity is desirable among the recipients of the second kind of religious education. Moran sympathises with Catholic leaders who desire to have members of their Church understand their own religion before encountering other religions, but he is adamant that understanding involves comparison. Dunne holds a similar position by advocating that by crossing over to other religions one comes back to one's own with much enrichment.[45] Moran extends his principle of comparison to the study of religion to include the mixing of young people of different faiths at university level, and in other appropriate contexts, for the purpose of understanding religion.[46]

This distinction made between the two types of religious education does not compartmentalise people into one or either category. Each recipient needs access to both kinds of religious education at the appropriate time in his or her life. It is possible or likely that there are times when both aims of religious education operate simultaneously, but at some moments in life one or the other is likely to dominate. For example, in early childhood, socialisation into the faith community necessarily takes precedence; in late adolescence there is usually a tendency to resist formation within the community, but if this tension is carefully facilitated, the mature adult can hold the two kinds of religious education in fruitful tension.

Despite the different forms of religious agency that are involved in the twofold religious enterprise, religious education already serves for both realities in different parts of the world. The world of the twenty-first century needs both faces of religious education. Moran argues that his comprehensive use of the term opens a fruitful dialogue between the two of them. It is not necessary for every religious educator to focus on both faces of this discipline, 'but while concentrating on one kind,' Moran says, 'the educator has to be aware of another aspect to the work'.[47] On the one hand, religious commitment does not preclude the importance of understanding religion and, on the other hand, scholars benefit from a feel for religious practice.

A religious education that embraces these contrasting activities of formation and understanding is threatened by opposite dangers. On one side, there is the danger that those who engage in a purely academic examination of religion would take over the meaning of the term, leaving religious bodies bereft of a link between internal cultural formation and the outside world's educational efforts in religion. This problem is associated, primarily, with countries such as Great Britain where the term religious education, especially at post-primary level, is usually confined to the designation of a subject taught in state schools. This danger does not exist in the United States and, until recently did not threaten the Republic of Ireland. In the latter case, however, this is changing as the study of religion becomes a subject in the curriculum of Irish secondary schools. This not only limits religious education to the school setting, but encapsulates it in one particular form. The opposite danger exists in the United States where religious education is regarded as an activity proper to a religious body, but illegal in the public school. A framework for a discussion on religion and education is badly needed in the United States. In this regard, the Catholic Church, which fueled the renewal of the term religious education since the Second Vatican Council, needs to be careful not to speak and act as if it owns the term.

In this respect, it must be acknowledged that the Catholic Church has the right and the duty to preserve its own language. The exclusive association of religious education with catechesis, however, contrasts it to a small and segregated part of the Church's ministry. This confining type of language diminishes the possibility of healthy educational discussion within the Catholic Church as well as the Church's association and dialogue with other educational bodies.

The words 'catechist' and 'catechise', which had their roots in the early Church and in early Protestant history, resurfaced after the Second Vatican Council. The use of these words is valid as a language of intimacy within Catholicism, but it should be kept in tension with language that transcends the Catholic Church. Catechesis, the aim of which is to form people in the Christian way of life, should not be burdened with the assumptions of the classroom. Likewise, academic religious education should not be burdened with the role of catechising. The type of teaching that occurs in the context of a homily or in sacramental preparation may be inappropriate in the classroom. In the academic sector, religion is taught whereas the catechetical venture focuses on the formation of people in a Christian way of life.

Moran's view of the catechetical as a small, but important, aspect of Catholic religious education is not reflected in Church documents or in most of the writing in this area over the past three decades. He believes that 'the catechetical aspect of the Catholic Church tends to overreach its place within the ministries of the Church'.[48] He disagrees that the tasks of the catechist are 'to proclaim Christ's message, to participate in efforts to develop community, to lead people to worship and prayer, and to motivate them to serve others'.[49] Only one of these, the proclamation of the message, clearly belongs to the catechist. Catechesis seems to be overreaching its task and role. This catechetical language needs to be complemented by an educational language. The educational formation of a Catholic rests more on worship and service than on catechetics. 'One learns to be a Catholic,' Moran writes, 'by participating in the liturgical life of the community'.[50] If educational reform is to be successful in the church, it must shift its concentration beyond catechisms, CCD, and textbooks.

Relating the Two Aims

The marriage of the two aims of religious education takes place in the person of the learner. Although one or other aim takes precedence at different stages throughout a person's life, it is hoped that every individual has the opportunity to engage in both aims. Like all education, religious education begins from the first moment of life, with the family being the natural setting for this first phase. As the child matures and develops, varying institutional contexts are available commensurate to the needs of age. While the first aim of religious education predominates in early childhood, the second aim is likely to become centre stage in adolescence as the facility to form abstractions occurs through conceptual and linguistic development. Both aims ought to characterise adult life.

In Moran's conceptualisation, therefore, religious education has a dual nature: formation in being religious and understanding religion. Thus, in conclusion, it can be said that the fullest understanding of religious education is:

> teaching people religion with all the breadth and depth of intellectual excitement one is capable of and teaching people to be religious with all the particularity of the verbal and nonverbal symbols that place us on the way.[47]

Where To From Here?
Perhaps a helpful way forward is to suggest some educational principles or guidelines that would enable us to unveil a truer meaning of religious education:

1. Attention must be paid to consistent educational clarity in the use of the term 'religious education'.
2. It is imperative to recognise the two very distinct, but interdependent, aims of religious education: to understand religion and the formation of a person into a religious way of life.
3. While both aims can be mutually supportive, these two processes of religious education – the academic process and the formation process – are very different and, therefore, have very different aims, objectives and purposes.
4. It is essential to recognise the different settings for religious education – the classroom is where one is taught to understand religion, while the parish and family settings are where one is taught to be religious.
5. Central to religious education is attention to lifestyle, a lifestyle that involves formation towards a virtuous character.
6. All religious education is education towards adulthood, that is towards psychological, social and religious maturity – in other words towards the Kingdom of God.

In summary, then, this chapter has examined the identity of religious education and the corpus of Gabriel Moran's writings has been the vehicle for unveiling the richest possible meaning of religious education for our time.

Notes

1. G. Moran, *Design for Religion* (New York: Herder & Herder, 1971); *Two Languages of Religious Education*, The Living Light, 14, pp, 40-50; *No Ladder to the Sky* (San Francisco: Harper & Row, 1987a); *Religious Education as a Second Language* (Birmingham, Alabama: Religious Education Press, 1989).

2. K. Scott, *Three Traditions of Religious Education*, Religious Education, 79, 1984, pp. 323-339.

3. F. Cunnane, *New Directions in Religious Education*, (Dublin: Veritas, 2004).

4. G. Moran, *Religious Body*, (New York: The Seabury Press, 1974), p. 150.

5. Ibid, p. 150.

6. G. Moran, *Where now, what next? Foundations of Religious Education*, Edited by P. O'Hare (Mahwah, NJ: Paulist Press, 1978).

7. G.A. Coe, *A Social Theory of Religious Education*, (New York: Shocken, 1917), p. 80, Original work published 1909.

8. C. Ellis Nelson, *Where Faith Begins*, (Atlanta, GA: John Knox Press, 1971), p. 38.

9. G. Moran, *Interplay* (Winona, MN: St Mary's Press, 1981), p. 159.

10. G. Moran, *Religious Education as a Second Language* (Religious Education Press, 1994).

11. Ibid, p. 9.

12. Ibid, p. 25.

13. Ibid, p. 105.

14. P.J. Palmer, *To Know As We Are Known* (New York: McGraw-Hill, 1983), p. xi.

15. G. Moran, *Understanding Religion and Being Religious*, PACE 21, 1992, pp. 249-252.

16. Ibid, p. 249.

17. C. E. Nelson, *Where Faith Begins* (John Knox Press, 1986).

18. J.H. Westerhoff, *Will Our Children Have Faith?* (New York: The Seabury Press, 1976).

19. J.H. Westerhoff and G. Kennedy Neville, *Generation to Generation* (New York: The Pilgrim Press, 1974).

20. B. Marthaler, *Socialization as a Model for Catechetics*, Foundations of Religious Education, Edited by P. O'Hare (New York: Paulist Press, 1978).

21. C. E. Nelson, *Where Faith Begins*.

22. Ibid, p. 40.

23. Ibid, p. 65.

24. Ibid, p. 155.

25. J.H. Westerhoff, *Will Our Children Have Faith?* (New York: Seabury Press, 1976).

26. J.H. Westerhoff and G, Kennedy Neville, *Generation to Generation* (New York: Pilgrim Press, 1974).

27. Ibid, p. 41.

28. Ibid, p. 46.

29. B. Marthaler, 'Socialization as a Model for Catechetics', *Foundations of Religious Education*, Edited by P. O'Hare (New York: Paulist Press, 1978).

30. J.H. Westerhoff, *Will Our Children Have Faith?*

31. M. Harris & G, Moran, *Reshaping Religious Education* (Louisville, KY: Westminster/John Knox Press, 1998), p. 30.

32. G. Moran, *Understanding Religion and Being Religious*.

33. J.H. Westerhoff and G. Kennedy Neville, *Generation to Generation*.

34. Ibid, p. 30.

35. Ibid, p. 43.

36. M. Harris and G. Moran, *Reshaping Religious Education* (Louisville, KY: Westminster/John Knox Press, 1998).

37. J.H. Westerhoff and G. Kennedy Neville, *Generation to Generation*.

38. G. Moran, *Understanding Religion and Being Religious*.

39. G. Moran, *Interplay*, p. 73.

40. Ibid, p. 73.

41. J.H. Westerhoff, *Will Our Children Have Faith?*

42. G. Moran, *Interplay*, p. 74.

43. Ibid, p. 154.

44. Ibid, p. 155.

45. J.S. Dunne, *The Way of All the Earth* (Notre Dame: The University of Notre Dame Press, 1978).

46. G. Moran, *Religious Education After Vatican II, Open Catholicism: The Tradition at its Best*, Edited by D. Etrymson & J. Raines (Collegeville, Minnesota: The Liturgical Press, 1997a).

47. Ibid, p. 156.
48. Ibid, p. 160.
49. National Conference of Catholic Bishops, *Sharing the Light of Faith, National Catechetical Directory for Catholics of the United States* (Washington, DC: National States Catholic Conference, 1979, No. 213).
50. G. Moran, *Religious Education After Vatican II, Open Catholicism: The Tradition at its Best*, p. 162.
51. G. Moran, *Understanding Religion and Being Religious*, p. 252.

Chapter 3

The Schoolteacher's Dilemma: To Teach Religion or Not To Teach Religion?

KIERAN SCOTT

I offer these reflections as an outsider, but a sympathetic outsider, to the issues of religious education in Ireland. My aim here is to provide an international perspective on some key issues currently confronting Irish endeavours. This international perspective will attend to variations in religious education within the English speaking world.

No international consensus currently exists on a comprehensive meaning of religious education – its nature, scope and purpose.[1] However, if we follow the actual use of the term by people who are committed to doing various activities under its rubric, religious education takes two forms or directions.[2] The first direction is illustrated by the United States. In the US, religious education is identified with religious groups. Religious education here teaches students to be religious in a, for instance, Roman Catholic, Protestant, Jewish way of life. This historical expression of religious education will be the focus of the next chapter.

In England and Wales, a different direction for religious education emerged in the 1940s. The 1944 Education Act defined religious education as comprised of two strands: worship and religious instruction. However, with the passage of time, dissatisfaction with collective worship in the school has thrown the meaning of religious education on to the second element, namely religious instruction. John Hull, one of the leading proponents of this shift observes: 'Religious education is no longer to foster or nurture faith in any particular religion; it is to promote a sympathetic but critical understanding of religion.'[3] Religious education here is to teach religion. It is spoken of as the subject of classroom instruction in the state school. This clearly defined academic venture has acquired a status in the school curriculum alongside other disciplines. This modern expression of religious education is the focus of my attention in this chapter.

As an added preface here, the Irish may be in a unique position to integrate both directions in religious education. In this period of fundamental cultural transition, I believe, they have the opportunity to adopt the best elements of each meaning. Ireland is one of the few places where both English and US writings on religious education are seriously attended to. What is seen as valuable from both sources can be combined with a distinctive Irish outlook on spirituality, the arts and education. To assist in this understanding, I will begin by examining the direction taken in Britain, namely, defining religious education as the teaching of religion.

There is hesitation, confusion and perplexity across the world, and, I believe, in Ireland also, as to what to do with religion. Reactions vary; in some settings, there is fear of evangelising. While in others, it is explicitly assumed and advocated. In some circles, the meaning of 'to teach religion' is understood as a confessional (catechetical) or even indoctrinative act. In other circles, the meaning is nearly the reverse, or simply a blur. The situation is not unique to Ireland or the US.

Three Case Studies

Three brief examples or case studies will illustrate the muddled confusion. Like a good movie reviewer, I will hold in abeyance the conclusion of each plot so as to lure you into my narrative.

1. In the Spring semester of 1994, I was assigned to teach a course entitled, *Toward a Theology of Christian Marriage*, on the undergraduate level. Some thirty-five students enrolled. My operating assumptions were: the setting is a classroom in a school; the content for engagement is marriage from a Christian perspective; the process is academic discussion and critique. Shortly before mid-term, I discovered not everyone shared my assumptions. We had just completed a unit on sexuality. The text is standard in the progressive and liberal theological tradition.[4] A student approached me a few days before mid-term examinations. He expressed his opposition to the text, its ideological framework and viewpoints. Confessionally, he was a devout, practising evangelical. The text was a source of temptation, he claimed. It was antagonistic to his fundamental hermeneutic. After consultation with his local minister, he requested exemption from the mid-term examination and exemption from studying the text.

This stimulated my thinking and became a catalyst for self-inquiry. What is at stake in teaching religion? What is involved in learning religion? From the teacher's perspective, is it work of advocacy? From the student's side, is it confessional confirmation? Or is it something else?

2. In August 2001, upon his appointment as the new Archbishop of Newark, New Jersey, John J. Meyers, gave an interview to the local newspapers throughout the state of New Jersey. One reporter inquired of the incoming Archbishop, who has a reputation as a staunch conservative, whether the faithful of the Archdiocese could question some official (but hotly debated) Church teachings. 'Yes, of course', replied the Archbishop, 'as long as they know we have the answers'. This unambiguous reply also stimulated my thinking and enquiring.

What do we mean when we say: 'The bishop is the chief teacher in the diocese'? Does he teach by being the primary guardian of doctrinal orthodoxy ('correct believing')? Are his teaching forms compatible or conflictual? Are they simply variations within a common and assumed confessional stance? Or are they not? Does the teaching act change according to settings? Does the teaching of religion depend on the mission of the school?

3. During my graduate studies, I enrolled in an intensive inter-session course. It was a deep and rapid immersion into the subject-at-hand. It was also a good way to quickly add three credits to one's transcript! The course topic was *Sexuality and the Social Order*. The course would change my life and world-view. First, I had the experience of being a minority. I was one of the four men in a class of thirty-one. Second, the course was my introduction to feminism and feminists. It was an experience in transformational learning.

One element in the course, however, unsettled me. As the classes progressed, assigned texts tended to be left aside. A personalistic group pedagogy took over. It represented a turn to the subject. The importance of personal experience as a source of knowledge was recognised. Permission and encouragement were given to self-expression, self-revealing, emotional unloading and confessional declarations. Psychic turmoil, sexual violence, emotional hurts, incest and sexual ambiguity were shared with all. In retrospect, it seemed like a forerunner to some current afternoon US talk shows. At one stage, the professor asked the four men to excuse themselves from the class because the women had 'female stuff to work on'. As the course turned more into a form of therapeutic encounter, I felt more ill-at-ease. The dynamics seemed more appropriate in a counselling setting or in a church confessional.[5]

This was also a catalyst for self-reflection. Is the classroom the place to work on psychic turmoil? Is it an arena for acts of confession? Can we replace the school desk with the psychologist's couch? Is classroom teaching a therapy session? What kind of space is the classroom? Is it a place where personal issues are traded for consolation? Or is it something else?

This chapter will attempt to unclutter, distinguish and clarify the issues at stake in the three examples noted. The focus of my attention is to uncover the meaning(s) of 'to teach religion'. The technology of teaching does not claim my primary interest here; nor does the disposition of the learner/student to learn; nor does the impact of social and cultural forces on the teaching-learning situation. These are, of course, vital components to consider in every educational context. But I wish to look at the issues from the other side, that is, from the perspective of the teacher, or to be more precise, from the side of the act of teaching. I will explore the meaning of the verb 'to teach' and its object 'religion' as they intermingle, interplay and intersect in contemporary schooling. But linking teaching and religion may not be as simple as it sounds. We can easily take a wrong turn and find ourselves in a mist of confusion. The complexity and ambiguity of the relationship between the two must be acknowledged. And the barriers on the road to their integration need naming and engaging.

Three Resistances to Connecting Religion and Education

The attempt to bring faith and learning (or religion and education) together in the modern classroom faces formidable obstacles. This attempt is comparatively new. It is a product of the twentieth century, and a child of the West. As one more preface to our discussion, the obstacles and resistance to this undertaking need to be faced. I will name three that have emerged, particularly in religious contexts and institutions, and in contemporary culture.[6]

The first problem originates in religion itself. Religion, understood as an internal conviction (faith), a piety, and a way of life makes its primary appeal not to the intellect (mind) by the affections (emotions). The vitality of religious faith is carried by individuals in passions, desires and powerful convictions. George W. Bush framed his politics after September 11 as a religious crusade for freedom. The Taliban did likewise with their holy war declarations. 'Islamic faith', the Taliban declared 'is a bright light: we seek to be so close to it that we catch fire'. Religiousness is full of zeal, if not at times fanaticism. It is 'hot stuff' – and any attempt to get a distance on it, to cool it down and engage in objective, dispassionate thinking, is viewed with suspicion in some churches, mosques and synagogues. Yet, that is precisely the task of the teacher of religion.

The second obstacle or resistance to connecting faith (religiousness) and learning has its roots in the (practice of the) religious or devotional life itself. The religious person yearns for the simple and the settled. The religious devotee seeks to be consoled, secured, rooted in ultimate meaning. Through proclamation, doctrines, sacred writings, moral dictates and rituals, this foundational footing is secured. This content is generally presented in modes of certainty and with cognitive security by church officials and their representatives. On the other hand, what does classroom teaching and learning offer? It too, offers resistance, but resistance to certitude, resistance to cognitive and imaginative closure. Through its process of inquiry, it opens up complexity and ambiguity. It reminds us that things may not be as simple as they appear. The classroom teacher offers an invitation: 'Let us go in search of deeper and richer understanding'. That invitation can create tension with institutionalised religion and its official representatives. But that is precisely the task of the teacher of religion.

The third obstacle or resistance to linking faith and learning (or religion and education) comes from the impact of post-modern culture on our schools. The following quote is from 1964, but I feel it is still relevant today:

> School teaching and learning in our advanced industrial society appears more and more as a matter of dispensing and acquiring of information rather than understanding. We have seen a shift in focus towards vocationally relevant skills and useful technical methods. We have come to value technique over tradition, skills over ultimate concerns, and information over understanding. Religion, on the other hand, involves tradition, symbols, written texts, mysterious practices and a variety of modes of understanding.[7]

It is not easy to get a hearing on that level or realm of meaning in our technical, driven climate. Religion in the school curriculum can seem a burden or an irritant, especially in the midst of an all-consuming Celtic Tiger. But once again, this is the vital and prophetic task of the teacher of religion.

These are formidable obstacles to the teaching of religion in our schools. Is the task, then, too much? Is the topic too hot? Is the process too tension-filled? Should we simply hand the work over to the churches and parishes? And if we did, would they be up to the task?[8]

I wish to make the case that the teaching of religion in our schools is one of the most universal, most urgent and most practical questions confronting our society today. The events of 11 September 2001 and its aftermath reveal that the main conflict in the world today is religious. Religion is not an innocent or a neutral force on the stage of history. The key question confronting us is: Will it be a life-giving force or will it turn deadly? A good starting point would be to seek to understand it. This is the unique contribution the teacher of religion can make to the current and the next generation. But, a prior and primary question, and the focus of our attention here is: What does it mean to teach religion? I will begin to decode this term by unveiling the meaning of the verb 'to teach', in its various forms, and with a particular focus on classroom teaching(s) in schools.

The Moral Dilemma of Teaching[9]

Teaching is an important test case of whether or not we understand what education is.

I think at some level, we are uneasy with the very idea of teaching. At a philosophical level we sense a moral dilemma in the idea of teaching. We have a deep suspicion that it is an immoral activity. Philosophically speaking, teaching is equated with the exercise of power by an adult over a vulnerable child. It is identified with a powerful adult trying to control the thinking of a powerless neophyte. We identify with telling the young the truth. In educational literature, it is assumed that teaching is an explanation from the front of the classroom. It becomes confused with a certain arrangement of power – one of great inequity.

The initial turn toward solving the moral dilemma of teaching is the recognition of the variety of teaching acts. Parents teach. Preachers teach. Schoolteachers teach and chaplains teach. But not all in the same way. It may be helpful to focus on the act of teaching and to ask: What exactly does a teacher do when engaging in the act? What kind of teaching is (or should be) going on here? What pattern of speech is (or should be) employed in this setting? Does it fit?

So before a teacher begins to teach, he or she needs to ask 'Why are these people in front of me?' The question is critical for each teacher, parent, coach, preacher, counsellor, kindergarten teacher, teacher of religion, university professor. Under what assumptions are these people present? What kind of licence to speak have they given me? What is appropriate (moral)? What is inappropriate (immoral)? The basis on which an individual or group appears before a teacher signifies a moral consent to a particular form of teaching and discourse. Much of the misunderstanding surrounding the term 'to teach religion', I believe, arises when people are confused about the nature of the institution they are in. Why are they assembled? What have the consented to? What language form is operating? Toward what is it directed? When the answer to these questions is unclear and distorted, the consent of the people gathered in front of the teacher is sometimes blurred and the teacher him- or herself may also be somewhat confused. The focus of our attention here, however, is the schoolteacher, specifically the teacher of religion, and the language appropriate to this task and setting.

School Teaching and Academic Speech
The classroom of the modern school is a unique invention. It structures a specific set of conditions that may be difficult to establish outside a school. It is designed for a particular pattern of language, namely, academic discourse. Academic speech is the use of speech for critical understanding. The schoolteacher employs academic discourse to turn speech back on itself and to investigate its assumptions, biases and meanings. Academic speech is disinterested speech. It is not partisan and preachy. To engage in it, we temporarily put on hold our involvement and convictions, as far as we are capable, to examine assumptions, contexts, blind spots. On the other hand, the schoolteacher is an advocate. He or she advocates how to speak so that greater understanding is possible. If the schoolteacher succeeds, students may reshape the pattern of their discourse, and, in effect, redesign their world and thus expand their awareness.

The schoolteacher, then, does not tell people what to think. And school teaching is not an exercise in truth telling. It is an invitation to examine the students' way of speaking and understanding. The words of the teacher and assigned texts are placed between the teacher and student. The ground rules are civility and tolerance. Everything else is open to critique. No opinion or viewpoint is uncritically accepted as truth. The assumption is every statement of belief, every linguistic expression of truth and every viewpoint can be improved upon. This saves the process from being authoritarian or indoctrinate.

The classroom, then, is a place for a particular kind of discourse, nothing more and nothing less. Discussion often takes the form of debate. There is a sense of back and forth, a dialogue, with a reflective use of language. Particular attention, however, is directed to the meaning of the words in the dialogue. The dialogue, as an oral exchange, can only bear fruit if the participants are willing to listen to the words of the other, and the voice and otherness of the assigned text. Written texts (or teacher, or students) that tend to preach or to be dogmatic defeat the purpose of the classroom. Good texts (or teachers, or students) need to leave open the possibility of imagining different viewpoints and alternative worlds. Classroom discussion then is the (inter)play of ideas. This approach to teaching honours the post-modern sensibilities outlined in chapter one.

In this linguistic framework, classrooms are designed to teach people to be sceptical. They are places to cultivate an attitude of questioning everything. They are arenas of criticism. The established world or assumed truth can be called into question. The verbal dialogue is between the teacher and the students. Both are participants, and both dialogue with the written (oral or visual) text. Teachers and students are invited to place their (informal) words on the table. Their words become the focus of attention and criticism. The classroom search is to understand the words on the table between teachers and students. The task is to distinguish meanings in a way that opens up and leads to greater understanding. The teacher does not simply describe or prescribe. He or she does not try to change the student or the student's thinking, only the student's words. The teacher is an advocate, but the advocate is for a better way of speaking. The schoolteacher's job is to propose a reshaping of the student's words. That is what is appropriate and academically permissible. This is what it means to teach morally in the classroom of the school.[10]

Academic speech, then, is concerned with meaning, with intellectual understanding. It questions the adequacy of every form of expression. Its form is interrogative. This critique, if it has communal support (within and outside the school), does not end in negativity. Rather, it can facilitate the emergence and flowering of new meaning and richer understanding. This is the purpose of classroom teaching. Consequently, when debate and criticism are absent, the classroom is simply not functioning as a genuine classroom.

When a student, then, enters a classroom in a school, he or she enters into a particular kind of discourse, namely academic speech. The schoolteacher is obliged to make it accessible. While academic discourse can emerge outside the school, the classroom in the school is particularly designed for it. Whether the school is a school of the Church (synagogue or mosque) or state school does not alter these assumptions. The school-teaching act is designed for discussion of ideas and their presuppositions. The teacher and students are partners (but not peers) in searching or researching the truth. If the right conditions prevail, the dialogue goes back and forth. The purpose is to move closer to the truth but without fixity, finality or absolutising. The teacher's first and last questions of concern are: What do the words mean? Who says so? Why? What are the assumptions? Is there a better way of saying that? The teacher, as advocate, shows and proposes a better way of how to do it. In the right place and time, this form of speech can be a powerful form of teaching, both morally appropriate and educationally counter-productive.

However, when these conditions are absent, academic discourse (schooltalk) can be educationally ineffective and morally offensive. A liturgical assembly is not the place for academic discussions. A therapist's office, for the most part, is not suitable for academic criticism. Academic discourse, like every other language, presumes a community. One cannot begin or end with criticism. But when teachers of religion ignore academic discourse, beliefs become dogmatic, interpretations closed and traditions idolatrous. When these conditions prevail, the classroom has ceased to function as a genuine classroom of the modern school and flies in the face of contemporary culture.

I will turn now to the task of connecting the verb 'to teach' with its object 'religion'.

Religion: An Academic Construct

In the title of this chapter, 'religion' is the direct object of the verb 'to teach'. In twentieth-century English, religion has two distinct and very different meanings: 1) It is a word for a set of practices that particular communities engage in. These (religious) communities, with their beliefs, rituals and moral practices, show a way of life. Religion here is what one lives and practices. 2) Religion is also a word to designate a field of academic inquiry.[11] It is an object of scholarly and academic investigation. It is the name of a curriculum subject. It represents stepping back to examine and understand these practices. Both meanings are well-established today. The second meaning is the focus of my attention here.

As a field of inquiry, religion is an idea and a concept that was invented in scholarly circles. It is an academic construct – like history, mathematics, social studies, health sciences. It was adopted as a neutral term by scholars who sought to study and compare particular religious communities. The focus and aim was to understand religion. But one can understand only if one compares. The concept implies understanding one (or one's

[handwritten margin note: Children don't understand academic construct atheist = no point / Belongs in school when taught correctly]

er possibilities. This is
an be a subject in the
psychology, politics or
) and as a method (of
se the mind in search
ate the muscles of the
critique.

form of inquiry? The
ly one place where it
the classroom of the
school. There is no place where religion more comfortably fits than in the academic curriculum. One preaches the Christian message, but one academically teaches religion. The schoolteacher steps back from the practice of the Christian (Jewish or Buddhist) ways of life so as to examine Christian (Jewish or Buddhist) beliefs, sacred writings and practices.

The aim is not change of behaviour, but change in understanding. This meaning of religious education flourishes in England and Wales and other parts of the world influenced by the UK. We have much to learn from this British model. Variations within this experience, from the phenomenological approach to the existential approach, to an integration of both, can be a rich source of educational wisdom for the rest of the world.[12] In terms of age, this process could begin with older children, increase during the teenage years, and reach its full fruition during the adult years. The teacher here is the schoolteacher. And the subject is religion. In (post)modern times, this form of religious education is indispensable to peace and harmony in the world.

School, then, is precisely where religion belongs. When it is taught, it fosters religious literacy, cultivates religious understanding and lessens religious prejudice. While schools carry all the burden for the formation and the development of a religious way of life, nevertheless, its limited contribution is vital to intelligent religiousness today.

Are our Christian Churches committed to the teaching of religion in their schools? Are they hospitable to the idea and method? Or are they suspicious and defensive? Catholic and Protestant communities give a prominent place to teaching. What is to be taught, and how it is taught, however, is usually very restricted. One is expected to teach the Word of God (Bible), Christian Doctrine, the catechism and the (moral) way. Traditionally, however, the method of teaching is by proclamation (preaching) and (catechetical) instruction. The Christian Churches have largely inherited this educational model. Education is viewed here as initiation, incorporation, induction into the faith. It is a process of religious socialisation, enculturation and maturation in the faith. On this, Catholic and Protestant communities generally have a consensus; Church education is teaching with an end in view. Their end is to produce practising Church members. However, schools and teaching religion in school have a different purpose.

Classroom instructors in religion have to examine what motivates their teaching. What have students consented to? What languages are appropriate? What assumptions are operating? What processes prevail? Teachers of religion in a school have to maintain the integrity of their own work. If religion is a part of the school curriculum, there is an academic standard to be met. Academic instruction should not be burdened with the role of catechising. The child who walks into the classroom of a school has the right to expect not catechising, but intellectually demanding accounts of religion – one's own and the religious way of the other. School teachers work in the context of the classrooms and an academic curriculum. Catechists work in their context of sacramental life. School teachers teach religion; catechists teach Gospel and Christian doctrine. Schools, whether government sponsored or religiously affiliated, attend to symbols, practices and documents. The catechetical venture is firmly within the framework of forming people to lead a Christian life. The teacher of religion is not a catechist. He or she is an academic teacher. Professionally, this is his or her identity. In religious terminology, this is his or her vocation.

Church officials, however, usually get uneasy and show some concern here. Will the teacher of religion 'present clearly what the Church teaches', or 'what the magesterium teaches'? Clearly that is what the catechist (or preacher) is commissioned to do. But it is the schoolteacher's task to 'present clearly what the school teaches'? The answer, in brief, is yes, if the material is relevant to the class topic of the day. But, in the teaching of religion, this is a preliminary step in school teaching. The next move or step is for the schoolteacher to ask: What does teaching mean? Where did it come from? What are its limitations? How is it changing? And dozens of similar questions. A schoolteacher's vocation is not to tell people what the truth is or tell them what to believe; a schoolteacher's modest task is to explore the meaning of what is written from the past and to help students articulate their own convictions. The truth or falsity of the Church's teaching is not a direct concern of the schoolteacher or student. This perspective tends to upset Roman Catholic officials. Their concerns are 'orthodoxy' and 'heresy'. These concerns, however, are on a different wavelength. Both words are irrelevant in the classroom. The teacher of religion teaches the subject matter. He or she teaches the student to think. He or she aids in the understanding of texts. What the student does with this understanding (affirm or dissent) is up to the individual student. The personal faith of the student or teacher is not an assumed part of the academic process nor its intended goal.

Three Teaching Tasks
Within this framework and set of assumptions, the first aim, in teaching religion is to make the material intelligible – or at least, to show how it is not unintelligible. The object to be

understood is religion, including one's own religion. Some degree of otherness, some basis of comparison is necessary to understand. The other reveals to us ourselves.[13]

The second task in teaching religion is to make the religious text accessible to students with 'disciplined intersubjectivity'.[14] The text is a mediator between the community of the past and a community of the present. The schoolteacher's job is to see that the text has a chance to fulfil that role. The discipline of the teacher here is the key. It must be done with fairness and fullness.

Thirdly, the teacher of religion must attend to classroom religion. The ecology and shape of the setting teaches. While the attitudes and personal interests of today's students cannot be the curriculum content, neither can these sensibilities and dispositions be ignored.[15] As soon as students step into the classroom space, they enter a zone of freedom. The space ought to be conducive to debate and critique. This teaching-learning design is indispensable if students are to discover the link between understanding (religion) and external (religious) practices. They must be free to choose.

Finally, I return to my initial three case studies and reveal the conclusion of each narrative. I did not exempt my Evangelical student from reading the assigned religion text or from sitting his examination. My aim, as a teacher of religion, in light of my foregoing argument, was not conversion, incorporation or indoctrination into a belief system, but rather an exploration and critical engagement of it. His responsibility, as a student, was to study and understand as best he could, but not necessarily believe. Whether the text was in accord with his conviction was irrelevant from an educational perspective.

Classroom instruction and Episcopal teaching are two different teaching forms, with two different purposes. They can be complimentary (not conflictual) when they respect each others territory and integrity. Bishops are called to teach by example. They are also guardians of orthodoxy. School teachers are also called to teach by example. However, their responsibility is neither to orthodoxy nor heresy. Their commitment is to the cultivation of understanding. What the student does with this understanding beyond the classroom wall is outside the realm of the teacher of religion. These two teachers and teaching forms ought to be in a healthy tension and conversation with each other. They should never be collapsed into one and the same. Finally, school-teaching is not therapy (although it may have therapeutic effects). Personal issues ought not be centre stage in the classroom. It is one thing to seek to make the material existentially relevant. It is quite another when the core material becomes an unloading of student's private wounds. Prudence, discernment and clarity of purpose ought never be lost sigh of in the classroom.

Ultimately, the teacher of religion is not a catechist or evangeliser for the Church. He or she is an advocate for intelligent understanding of one's own religious tradition in relation to other people. What's at stake is understanding ourselves better through appreciating other religious ways as best we can. The choice is between ignorance and empathy. The schoolteacher of religion chooses life, chooses enlightenment, chooses revelatory understanding. This is our sacred vocation.

Notes

1. See my *Three Traditions of Religious Education*, Religious Education 79, 3, 1984, p.323-339.
2. G. Moran, *Religious Education as a Second Language* (Birmingham, AL, Religious Education Press, 1989) p.226-242.
3. J. Hull, *New Directions in Religious Education* (London: Falmer Press, 1982), p.xiv.
4. J. B. Nelson, *Embodiment: An Approach to Sexuality and Christian Theology* (Minneapolis, MN, Augsburg, 1978).

5. On the risks of personalistic teaching technique methodologies, see K. Homan, 'Hazards of the Therapeutic: On the Use of Personalistic and Feminist Methodologies', *Horizons*, 24, 1997, p.248-264.

6. See E. Farley, 'Local Learning: A Congregational Inquiry', in M. Warren (ed.) *Changing Churches: The Local Church and the Structure of Change* (Portland, Oregon: Pastoral Press, 2000) p.138-161.

7. P. Phenix, *Realms of Meaning* (New York: McGraw Hill, 1964)

8. See G. Moran, Does 'Religion Belong in a Parish?' in *Religious Education as a Second Language* (Birmingham, AL: Religious Education Press, 1989) p.138-164.

9. I note my indebtedness in this section to the recent work of Gabriel Moran. See, in particular, his *Showing How: The Act of Teaching* (Valley Forge PA: Trinity Press International, 1997)

10. Ibid., 124-125.

11. Moran, *Religious Education as a Second Language*, p.123-124.

12. On these various approaches see J. Hull, *Studies in Religion and Education* (Lewes, Sussex: The Falwer Press, 1984); M. Grimmitt, *Religious Education and Human Development* (Great Wakering, Essex: McCrimmons, 1987); E. Cox, *Problems and Possibilities for Religious Education*, (London, Hodder and Stoughton, 1983); A. Wright, *Religious Eduction in the Secondary School: Prospects for Religious Literacy* (London: David Fulton, 1993)

13. See T. Veiling, *Emmanuel Levinas and the Revelation of the Other*, Eremos 61, 1997, p.23-25.

14. P. Phenix, 'Religion in Public Education: Principals and Issues' in D. Engel (ed.), *Religion in Public Education* (New York: Paulist, 1974), p.67.

15. See H. Lombaerts, *Religion, Society and the Teaching of Religion in Schools* in Michael Warren (ed.), Sourcebook for Modern Catechetics, Vol. 2 (Winona, MN: St Mary's Press, 1997) p.306-329 for some characteristics of the teaching of religion in the school environment in light of changes in the European continent.

Chapter 4

Continuity and Change in Religious Education: Building on the Past, Re-Imagining the Future

Kieran Scott

At the beginning of the previous chapter, I noted two distinct parts or directions religious education takes in the English-speaking world. These two faces of religious education[1] were captured for me in a cartoon I saw recently. Two psychics are seated with their crystal ball at their respective tables each side of a street corner. On the left side, one psychic advertises her wares, psychic reading $10: all of life's questions answered. On the right side, the other psychic advertises, psychic reading $10: all of life's answers questioned. In some caricatured way, these two pictures represent the two major sets of activities operating under the canopy of religious education on both sides of the Atlantic today. The former is the US practice. The latter is the UK one. I will seek in this chapter to show that they are not mutually exclusive. However, the former, for the most part, will be the focus of my attention.

In spite of the case I attempted to make in the previous chapter for the teaching of religion, schools alone cannot carry the entire burden and challenge of religious education. To concentrate exclusively on the religious instruction of children and adolescents within school settings is equivalent to a bird attempting to fly on one wing. It simply won't work. It is inadequate for a full, intelligent religious life. Although schooling in religion can have a short-term effect upon students (in terms of understanding), any lasting effect is discernable only when this schooling is reinforced by family ties, prayer ties, social outreach ties; that is, other diverse and complementary forms of religiously educative activities.

The future challenge, then, entails getting beyond (but not leaving behind) the schooling paradigm. Or, better stated, the task is to place the schooling in religion in a larger context of complementary educational forms of life. Put simply, effective teaching of religion in schools is dependent on the cooperation of parish, home and school. Each must be recognised as playing a role in education towards a mature religious life. The role of each will be distinctive and unique. Each needs affirmative nature and linkage with the other. When this is recognised, they can balance and complement each other.

As noted in chapter three, Ireland is in a particularly good position to adopt the best elements within a comprehensive meaning of religious education. In Ireland especially, we can see the tension between a traditional nineteenth-century form of Church[2] and all the currents of a contemporary post-modern culture.[3] The rebellion of Ireland's young people today against this traditional Church form, (with its Tridentine strategy and emphasis on obedience to rules), calls for the opening up of new and flexible tracks to access their lives.[4] This crisis of access ('people without a system') may challenge the existing institution to reclaim some of the richer elements of its own Celtic spiritual past. It may also challenge schools, Churches and families to incorporate some of the British and American forms and practices of religious education.

In the short run, this may give rise to a 'Babel of languages' in religious education discussion. In the long run, however, it could be seen as a genuine attempt to honour the two arms of religious education: the academic and the pastoral, the study and practice, the understanding and formation in a religious way. What is selectively adopted from these foreign sources could be combined with a distinctive Irish past and with present post-modern sensibilities. But the pivotal question is: How do we get there from here?

Building on the Past

If religious education is ever to flourish, its meaning cannot be separated from the past or from the existing work and loyalties of large numbers of people today.

Historically, religious education (if the term was used at all) was perceived as a way of inducting new members into the religious tradition of our ancestors. It was a way for the religious body to perpetuate itself. In modern times, many of these traditional processes and strategies have broken down. They have become dysfunctional.[5]

In response, religious communities (Roman Catholic, Protestant, Jewish) have adopted some of the techniques and methods of modern education to help them achieve the same end, namely, formation of the neophyte in the tradition. Even though this move tended to protect the religious tradition from rational criticism, there was something valuable to retain here: attention to the concrete, particular and mysterious practices of a religious tradition. The wisdom lay in showing (teaching) people how to be religious in a Roman Catholic, Protestant or Jewish way.

On the other hand, the most lucid meaning of religious education in the world today is outside of church settings. It is in government schools in England and Wales. Here, as noted above, religious education is the well-defined work of the professional schoolteacher. It is the name of the classroom subject. It is the teaching of religion. Likewise, there is something valuable to retain here, namely, systematic reflection on the practice of our religious ways. The wisdom is in showing (teaching) people how to understand their own tradition in relation to a set of practices of the other.

Both wisdoms can be building blocks to a re-imagined future. The key to the future, however, lies in their integration. The question is: can we attend to the concrete, traditional practices of religion and, simultaneously, honour the modern study of religion? Or are these two sets of activities fundamentally conflictual and compartmentalised? To attempt an integration is like balancing hot and cold, yin and yang, husband and wife. But this is precisely the marriage needed at this time and in this place. I will deal with the need for integration in the latter part of this chapter.

First, however, let me take up the ancient form of religious education with its concern for initiation and formation in a religious heritage. In the United States, this is the direction religious education has taken in the latter half of the twentieth century. In contemporary Ireland, this form of religious education has run into serious trouble. Religion as a chain of memory has been broken in this generation.[6] No religious community, however, can long sustain its life without a built-in educational process. No religious tradition can survive without reconnecting the chain of memory.

Education has to do with the maintenance of community through the generations – its preservation and improvement. This maintenance or conservation must assure enough continuity of vision and values to sustain the self-identity of the community. Education here offers continuity.

At the same time, this work of maintenance must honour freedom and novelty, if it is to be adaptable to new circumstances. Education here offers change. This dynamic interplay between continuity and change enables a religious tradition to avoid, on the one hand, becoming a fossil or simply irrelevant, or, on the other hand, disappearing into relativism. Preservation and improvement, traditioning and transformation, then, are the dual purpose of education. It has to do with form, re-forming and re-patterning the life forms of a people. Religious education, at its best, is that dynamic process operative in a religious body and its set of practices.

Where can we turn for assistance and guidance in incorporating these educational processes and strategies? Walter Brueggemann proposes that we may find clues for this type of education deeply rooted in our religious heritage. In his book, *The Creative Word*,[7] Brueggemann draws attention to the process and shape of the Old Testament biblical canon. How the biblical material reached its present form (canonical process) and the present form that it has reached (canonical shape) offers, he claims, insight into the community's self-understanding and its intent for the coming generations. His thesis is: this canonical process and construct models, both in terms of substance and as a process, educational ministry in our churches.

But what is the canonical process we discern? It is one of stability and flexibility, continuity and discontinuity, formation and re-formation, tradition and re-interpretation. And what is the canonical structure? The construct is the tripartite canon: law (Torah), Prophets, Writings.[8] In ancient Israel, it was this construct or shape that permitted and articulated the dynamic of continuity and change. The people of Israel valued all three parts of the canon. They held them in relational tension to each other. They were clear about the place and function of each, and never tried to make one substitute for another. Brueggemann directly implies that this threefold structure and principle of continuity and change tells us what to look for in parish religious education today.

I will turn now to these biblical texts and themes and view them through an educator's lens and interests. Each of the three parts of the canon has a different function. Each offers different forms of knowledge. Each has a different agent of instruction. And, each makes different claims to us. Conservatives, social critics and liberals may – by personal inclination and conviction – be drawn toward one part of the canon or another to the relative neglect of the others: conservatives toward Torah, social critics toward the prophets: liberals toward 'the counsels of the wise' (Writings). However, a faithful community and integrated religious education must attend to all three. As Brueggemann remarks, 'Church education, both in its models and its substance, has gone awry precisely because of the failure to hold these three parts of the canon, these three normative modes of discourse, in balance and tension.'[9]

Critical of this endeavour will be the honouring of different teaching forms. The three (biblical) educational agents are the priest, the prophet and the sage. The three processes of education they unleash are: disclosure of what binds us as a people – the priestly task/role; disruption of the established order and critique of our wayward ways – the prophetic task/role; disruption of some fundamental order and meaning in our lives – the sage's task role.

Religious education in its fullness creates educational space for each pedagogical form. As I proceed, I will correlate the tripartite canonical structure and the three teaching roles with contemporary forms of religious education. I will turn now to take up in some detail each part of the canon and illustrate the type of education it embodies and evokes.

Torah Education

The first accent or form of biblical education is Torah focused. Torah education is a process of nurturing and leading the new generation into a view of reality held by our forefathers and foremothers in the faith. Torah is a statement of community ethos – its story and vision. It is a definitional statement of the character of the community. Communal identity is first established by stating its parameters and boundaries, and perceptual field in which the neophyte must live and grow. Torah seeks to form consensus on what claims of memories and stories link people. It wants to disclose what values and visions bind a community in solidarity. This content and material is foundational for the educative forms to follow. It ushers the neophyte into a safe, secure life-world. In doing this, it saves the young from rootlessness, chaos, alienation and narcissistic subjectivity.

Torah education is education as nurture and formation. It deals with what is known, normative and given. It reports on that upon which there is consensus. It cultivates a centre for life, a core and chain of memory, an organising principle of life. One could say, it is the practice of the first naiveté (Ricoeur). It is essentially uncritical or precritical. It does not invite rational criticism. Rather its heremeneutic is one of retrieval and affection. With this focus, it provides the foundation for religious homecoming for children and adults. This form of religious education, then, is the formalised process of traditioning, the handing on of a way of life and its set of convictions to the next generation.

The primal mode of education, derived from Torah, is story. It is communal narration. The narrative offers a distinctive way of knowing. It is concrete, open-ended, experiential and the practice of imagination. As a retelling of Israel's public memory, it is subversive. It retrieves the 'dangerous memory' of a people, which, in turn, challenges an imperial consensus and offers a counter-cultural vision of reality. The story is to be told with charm, aesthetic sensitivity and partisan fidelity. This re-telling of a people's story keeps memories and hopes alive. It maintains religion as a chain of memory.

In contemporary Roman Catholicism, catechesis is the internal language for this form and process of educational ministry. Catechesis is the educational work of the Church, in the Church, and on behalf of the Church. It is unabashedly confessional. Its end in view is transmission of the heritage.

Catechesis is vigilant about its own borders. Its gift is in honouring the past, affirming religious roots and sustaining a rich sacramental life. This is the work of catechist, parent liturgist, and adult eductor.[10] It reminds one where one's home is and from what religious tribe one has sprung. This is its gift, but it is also its weakness. Its parochial language does not build bridges to other tribes – or other religious possibilities.

Catechesis, however, or Christian education as Protestants name it, is religious education in concrete expression. But how the elements of the tradition (teachings, rituals, practices) are approached will determine whether they are educational or not. Education is the re-shaping of religious traditions with end (purpose) and without end (closure).[11] Catechesis, as religious education, must fulfil both conditions. First, it must be education with an end in view (purpose). There is a way of life to be conveyed. There is a story to be told and made accessible. Second, *how* it is made accessible is key. The tracks must be laid down in such a way that the group recognises that there are truths beyond whatever has been formulated. If the catechist attempts to fix the mind on an established body of material that bears no further development, this would not qualify as education. It seems closer to socialisation or indoctrination. But, if, on the other hand, the catechist, in his or her every pronouncement, every ritual, every teaching, every belief and every gesture toward the other, acknowledges the community's incompleteness, this would qualify as education. In fact, it is among the most important priestly forms of religious education needed in the world today.

Prophetic Education

If we engage in Torah education (catechesis) we will do our people a great service. If a community, however, educates only in Torah, it may also do a disservice to its members. It may mature them to fixity, rigidity, to a sense that 'all questions are settled' and need only be recited (catechism style) over and over. This idealises the tradition, making it into an idol. Jaroslave Pelikan writes, 'Tradition is the living faith of the dead, traditionalism is the dead faith of the living. And... it is traditionalism that gives tradition such a bad name.'[12] Prophetic education is a call to resistance against traditionalism.

There are two moments in this prophetic process: criticising and energising.[13] It begins with the cultivation of suspicion and then moves toward the formation of an alternative imagination. In more technical terms, we would say: it commences with a hermeneutic of suspicion and proceeds to a hermeneutic of reconstruction. This prevents closure of judgement on the past and collapse of imagination in the future. These two movements or moments held in creative tension are the key to the vitality of prophetic education.

The first role of prophetic education is criticism. The task is to surface and foster critique that penetrates the numbness and staleness of the dominant culture or/and the religious tradition. Its work is to cut through, what Virginia Woolf called, 'the cotton wool of everyday life'. It does this by bringing a disruptive word to the established version of reality.

The function of the prophetic is to challenge the prevailing consensus, to practise criticism on that which until now has been beyond criticism. Prophecy is needed when we sense the old consensus is breaking down. It is urgent when the old truths have become inert, boring, weary, irrelevant, 'the dead faith of the living.' Prophetic education brings critique to the death-producing element of a people's story – its practices, doctrines, symbols and codes. The process is on developing the reflective consciousness of the total community with regard to the total community's life.

Education in the prophetic, then, means teaching people to take seriously, but not too seriously, official truth about fact, knowledge, power, interpretation. It is to be a catalyst for the surfacing of suspicion. This disruptive world is in the long and rich tradition of Jeremiah, Jesus, Martin Luther King and Paulo Freire. Paul Tillich, the great Protestant theologian, named this word and process 'the Protestant principle'. He described it as the need to question our certainties in the very moment when they become absolutely certain. It is a word of resistance to the absolutist instinct. It is education as protest against closure on life's meaning. No thing is God: no viewpoint, no code, no rite and no policy. The educational task here is to prevent the creation of new idols.

The second role of a prophetic approach is in energising. The prophets protest what is. But the protest does not end in negativity. It is also protest for what is promised, namely, fresh forms of life. The education task here is to stimulate an alternative imagination and energise the emergence of a renewed story. This is the work of a hermeneutic of restoration, fertilised by the power of the creative imagination. This educational moment creates new openings and fresh forms of faithfulness and vitality. New 'moments of being' (Virginia Woolf) are ushered in and 'the living faith of the dead' (Pelikan) re-directs our lives.

This accent of prophetic education can lead to the revitalising of religious tradition and create life-giving forms of social grace in our world. Its power is in proposing an alternative imagination that redefines our situation. This is a movement beyond critique into the language of creativity and amazement. The restlessness with old truths is left behind and the recreation of new truths breaks upon us. Prophets are religious poets. They bring the passion of God to speech. They speak new forms of life into being.

Prophetic education, then, honours deliberation and inquiry. It places priority on the critical and reconstructive rather than on proclamation and formation. It does more than simply tell. Its orientation is toward posing and opening up new perspectives. Torah offers safe limits. But the prophetic protest stretches and widens out our boundaries toward new realities.[14] In a word, prophetic education challenges every old truth for the sake of a new and richer truth which is breaking in upon us.

In contemporary Roman Catholic circles (and in liberal Protestant groups), the revisionist model of Christian religious education typifies this form of education. The work of Thomas Groome is a leading representative example of it.[15] Groome and his colleagues bring a critical hermeneutic to bear on the Christian tradition and correlate it with a critical decoding of contemporary human experience. This process is set to five educational movements by Groome and goes by the name of 'shared Christian praxis'.[16] It involves the application of modern critical reason to beliefs, symbols, values and lived-life of the Christian tradition. The process weds tradition and modernity, continuity and change. This enables the Christian tradition to become self-conscious – through the process of critical distancing. This form of education can save the tradition from dogmatism and traditionalism, and allow the creative re-appropriation of the heritage as a life-giving power. It can re-root us in the Christian tradition and allow us to live in creative tension with it.

This prophetic education belongs in the classrooms of our schools. The schoolteacher facilitates the re-interpretative task. This process also belongs at the centre of parish life. If the tradition is to come alive for people, all members need access to this educative form. It ought to be institutionalised into the structure of parish life and find multiple forums for expression. Something very fundamental is at stake here. Are we going to be conscious participants in the tradition or unconscious victims of it? The way we answer that question will tell us within a few generations whether we will have a tradition worth saving.

Wisdom Education

The third accent of religious education is neither disclosure (of the social glue that binds a people), nor disruption (of this cohesiveness), but rather discernment of our common human experience. Directing us in this discernment is the sage. The sage and the prophet do not start from the same premise, nor do they move in the same direction. They do not deny the legitimacy of the other's focus. They are complementary, not contradictory; each has its distinctive motifs.

The distinctiveness of wisdom education is the cultivation of a different kind of knowing. The concern is not just for knowledge we can acquire, but knowledge we must wait and listen for in ordinary life. The posture needed is patience, a respect for not knowing what is yet to be discerned, an honouring of mystery.

The pedagogical task here is to show how to discern, how to attend to gifts given in experience, how to be receptive to the world around us, how to listen to the voice of Mystery (Word of God) in creation, in human and animal behaviour, in the lilies of the field. In a way, it is education toward knowing that what we see is not all there is. It is education for life – everyday life – and for unveiling the ultimate meaning undergirding it.

This kind of education exposes the rational limits of most modern education. Knowledge is not just rationally acquired, and the human person is not only the passive recipient of knowledge. Knowledge can be *discovered* and the human can be the generator of new knowledge not known before. However, the fundamental stance is close to a religious one, namely humility.

According to the sage, those who engage in their ordinary life, with their eyes and ears wide open, will see and hear intimations of more. Wisdom education cultivates and celebrates this human capacity for receptivity. The writings seek to discern order and meaning in the minutiae of mundane living. The sage's final word is not critique, but one of wonder, awe and amazement: doxology. This prayerful word is premised in the holy interconnectedness of all things. This is the central substance of the wisdom teachers. And the way to discover this web of holiness is by delving into the depth of life. Wisdom education is revelatory. The sage shows us how to pull back the veil covering the spiritual dimension.

Wisdom literature is a loose and miscellaneous collection of writings. They resist easy categorisation – lacking cohesive themes or authoritative rigour. There are two main hypotheses about wisdom. On the one hand, it is argued that there is *clan wisdom*. Here the sage teaches the young in the ways of the tribe by an informal process of socialisation. The other hypothesis sees wisdom as (formal) instruction in the *court school*. Both can be commended and both can serve our purpose here. And both can be related to the two dominant literary types in instruction. One, commonly called, 'instruction', is intentionally didactic. It takes the form of imperatives and prohibitions. While the other form, the sayings, emerge out of a tradition of experience. It takes the form of everyday folk-wisdom. As a body, the wisdom literature deals more explicitly and seriously with educational concerns than other writings. As noted, some of its educational focus is intentionally didactic. In other writings, it is indirect and evocative. On the basis of this delineation, I will sketch out six education concepts found in the wisdom traditions.

The first basic educational principle of wisdom is the insistence that we pay close attention to our daily-lived experience. Daily life must be respected and honoured, but also carefully discerned. This is the curricular content and the focus of the sage's teaching. The mundane events of life with their joys and sorrows, work and leisure, loves lost and gained, when reflected upon, can lead to discerning powerful and pervasive truths. The sage directs the learner to move in and through his or her own experience to make sense and meaning of it all.

The sage is linked to a tradition, a chain of memory. His or her pervasive concern is to connect the tradition to the learner's own experience. Both must be honoured. Both will change and grow as the community's understanding deepens. When a vital connection is made, tradition can make life work.

Traditions are embodied in texts. At times, texts seem to be substitutes for us for dealing with life. On the other hand, for the sage the study of text is a means to study life. The text mediates between a community of the past and a community of the present. It extends 'the franchise to our ancestors' (Chesterton). It can be a source of ancient wisdom and human possibility.

Wisdom teaches us that there is a proper time for everything. The sage is concerned with what is educationally suitable – saying and doing the right thing, in the right place, with the right people. In the current terminology, we could call the sages developmentalists. They had an acute sense of educational readiness. This requires a sense of judgement, which is intellectual, ethical, aesthetic and psychological all at once. The effective religious educator needs this proper sense of timing in every educative setting.

In the wisdom traditions, the pedagogical process is inherently dialogical. The conversation goes between the divine and human, tradition and experience, word and deed, texts and people, young and old. The Book of Job, for example, is a story of conversational engagement. Job's engagement with God is highly contentious, argumentative, and passionately dialectical. Job would have performed well as a schoolteacher of religion – a process that calls for dialectical discourse. He was a provocateur of the mind and a catalyst of cognitive dissonance. He lived the questions. Effective religious educators create this intellectual friction by moving back and forth between speaking and listening. Its gift is to enable students (and teachers) to think outside the box and acquire new understandings.[17]

The teaching methods of sages do not rely exclusively on memorisation. They proceed by encouraging participation in the creative process. Ready-made answers and universal truths are not supplied. Rather, the process and style is more indirect and evocative: playful, childlike, humorous, paradoxical, a teasing into truth. Their tricks of the trade are puns, riddles, parables, stories, fables and imagery. This playing with knowledge helps to resist the lust for certainty and keeps open the hunger for wisdom. Consequently, the teaching of the sage, unlike priest and prophet, is just for today. It is partial and provisional. New future experience may enable us to make new judgements based on new data. Some will see, in the teaching of the sage, a post-modern strategy – an honouring of particularity, ambiguity and plurality. This premodern pedagogy may be timely for a post-modern education.

Finally, for the sage, education is not so much a process of dissemination of information or the mastery of knowledge, but the formation of character. Education is forming persons of integrity. Truth is not just thought, but action. The hypocrite is the fool. For the sage, a person is wise only when he walks wisely, only when he is a doer of the word. This congruence between word and deed is a life of integrity. It is also one of the ultimate purposes of religious education.

As it stands, on both Roman Catholic and Protestant sides, this form of religious education is comparatively undeveloped. Torah and prophetic educative forms hold centre stage. The recent writings of Charles Melchert have broken the mould on this genre and are a rich resource.[18] I would also interpret the later writings of Gabriel Moran within this kind of education.[19] Like a sage, for Moran, God is in the details of life. Revelation is a process of listening and seeing. Moran counsels: trust the authority of your experience, and gifts of reason, intuition and imagination. Don't wait around for officials to hand down the answers.

In Moran's project, religious education is directed to ordinary, everyday life. Its focus is the life of work, leisure, family and school. It seeks to bring us to a centre. This education begins with discerning life as good. It proceeds by evocatively calling us to re-shape it into a whole, namely, a life of holiness. In the final analysis, this distinctive type of education is designed to raise up wise men and wise women in our midst. Its ultimate goal is a wise people standing, walking and resting in the presence of the Wise One.

Seven Habits of Highly Effective Religious Education

Religious education is an educational approach to the religious life of children, adolescents and adults. In the English-speaking world, as I noted above, religious education has taken two major directions: immersion in a religious tradition and stepping back to study it. Currently, these two directions tend to locate people in separate compartments or parallel tracks. At their best, however, these two processes can be profoundly complementary and integrative. For a rich and intelligent religious life, people need access to each kind at some time in their lives. Both kinds can operate simultaneously in a person's life, although at different periods one is likely to predominate.

In the early years, teaching people to be religious, with the goal of formation into the religious group, will take precedence. In late adolescence and early adulthood, this formation process is often challenged. Teaching religion, with the purpose of understanding, needs to commence at this stage. The older adult is in the best position to maintain a fruitful tension between the two kinds of religious education.

Not every religious educator has to do both kinds of education. Some may wear both hats at different times in different settings. Some may concentrate on only one kind. While focusing on this one kind, however, the educator needs to be aware of the other complementary aspects of the work. The overall educational strategy and intention is to facilitate easy passage from one side to the other.

In brief summary form, I will identify three habits with each approach, and a seventh to tie them together.

Religious Education as Formation in the Practices of a Religious Community

The first habit of the religious educator is to show people how to root themselves in a religious heritage. Young and old need a place to stand, a religious home, and an underlying structure of meaning to support their lives. They need incorporation into tradition. Tradition is a set of enduring practices – attitudes, rituals, beliefs, disciplines and style of action. These practices need to be put on like one's clothing. They will be modelled foremost by parents. Tradition is also comparable to a living language. It has its grammar and rules. The initial task of the religious educator is to show the neophyte how to speak the language, in other words, how to embody the practices. This is religious education as catechesis.

Religious traditions, however, can become dead and deadening. They can become stale, rote and meaningless, and little more than a tourist curiosity. We have a choice – we can be conscious participants in the practices or unconscious victims of them. The choice is between (creative) recovery and (numbing) rejection.

The effective religious educator enables young and old to re-root themselves in their religious tradition by a process of critical appropriation. Interpretative skills are needed to do this: skills of critical reflection, critical remembering and creative reconstruction. These skills will enable the religious educator to show people how to revitalise a dormant religious heritage.

Religious education in Church and family ought to be an education by practice, that is, the practice of a vibrant religious life. The life of a parish and the practice of family living ought to show by its rituals, its modelling of virtue, its sense of sacramentality, its spirituality, its polity and its social outreach, a path of knowledge. They ought to educate by doing – showing a human way of living, dying and going beyond dying. The educator here is the whole communal life of parish and family. The parent, the priest, the catechist, the chaplain, the social activist, each with his or her own distinctive skills and in collaboration with each other, show the community how to walk the way.

This will require a re-shaping of Church – its communal life, its life of worship and its political structures so as to make possible a powerful Christian witness. A similar re-shaping of the family is needed for it to become a more effective educative form.

Religious Education as Teaching to Understand Religion

The effective religious educator directs students toward intellectual understanding. This should be done with fairness and integrity. The schoolteacher makes accessible a rich and deep knowledge of the tradition. He or she shows forth the tradition in a luminous manner. The style of showing, however, needs to be dialogical. The tradition has to be open to questioning. It is not an idol. It is good, but not God.

This teaching and study of religion must be inter-religious. Religious identity is powerful. It can bind, seal and close people off in a collective 'sameness'. This is sectarianism. A healthy and mature identity, however, springs from acquiring a sense of who I am in relation to who I am not. The other elicits my identity. The face of the other evokes my response and enriches my self-understanding. The effective teacher of religion enables students in classrooms to cross over into the (inner) world of the other and to return to their own religious world transformed. In this way, they can discover the deeper roots of their own heritage.

Schooling in religion is not just for school children. There is a critical need to involve adults in an educationally effective way. Before September 11, George W. Bush thought the Taliban was a contemporary rock group. A fundamentalist Muslim assumes and asserts it is the only authentic version of Islam. Similar claims are made by fundamentalist Christians, Jews, Hindus, in fact, almost all world religions. We see throughout the world today that ignorance can be deadly and destructive. Adult religious literacy is indispensable in our pluralistic religious world. It needs to be at the centre of the curriculum of parish religious education.

Partners in Interplay

The final habit for the effective religious educator is to place these two sides, the practice and study, in interaction with each other. This may be the most valuable habit and skill of all. Religious educators need to attend to this continuous engagement. Practice without study can become blind, narrow and meaningless. Whereas understanding without practice flies into abstraction, detachment and lack of appreciation. The religious educator brings them together as a couple in creative tension. In enabling this marriage, he or she points the way toward a mature religious way of being in the world. And this, I would claim, is the ultimate purpose of religious education... a religious education that honours continuity and change, that builds on the past and re-imagines the future.

Notes

1. See G. Moran, 'Religious Education after Vatican II' in D. Efroymson and J. Raines (eds.), *Open Catholicism: The Tradition at its Best* (Collegeville: Liturgical Press, 1997), p.151-166.
2. See M. Drumm, 'A People formed by Ritual', in E.G. Cassidy (ed.) *Faith and Culture in Irish Context* (Dublin: Veritas Publications, 1996).
3. See O. V. Brennan, *Cultures Apart? The Catholic Church and Contemporary Irish Youth* (Dublin: Veritas Publications, 2001) on how this tension is being played out in the lives of contemporary Irish youth.
4. M. Kennedy, 'Tracks into a New Civilisation: A View of the Irish Roman Catholic Church' in Michael Warren (ed.), *Changing Churches: The Local Church and the Structure of Change* (Portland: Pastoral Press, 2000): 90-108.
5. Ibid; Brennan, op. cit. and M. P. Gallagher, 'Atheism Irish Style' *The Furrow*, April 1984.

6. See D. Hervieu-Léger, *Religion as a Chain of Memory* (New Brunswick, New Jersey: Rutgers University Press, 2000)

7. W. Brueggemann, *The Creative Word* (Philadelphia, PA: Fortress, 1982).

8. The Torah, the first five books of the Old Testament, is called the Pentateuch. This literature embraces Genesis, Exodus, Leviticus, Numbers and Deuteronomy. The prophetic writings group together Joshua, Judges, Samuel and Kings – termed the 'former prophets' – and Isaiah, Jeremiah, Ezekiel – and the twelve (minor prophets) – termed the 'latter prophets'. The Wisdom literature, also named the Writings, is a miscellaneous collection of counsels. Of these various books, the most important are the Psalms, Job, Proverbs, Ecclesiastics and the Wisdom of Solomon.

9. Brueggemann, op. Cite, p.11.

10. K. Scott, 'Three Traditions of Religious Education', *Religious Education* 77, 6, 1982: pp.615-627.

11. G. Moran, *Religious Education as a Second Language* (Birmingham, Al: Religious Education Press, 1989), p.49.

12. J. Pelikan, *The Vindication of Tradition* (New Haven, CT: Yale University Press, 1984), p.65

13. W. Brueggemann, *The Prophetic Imagination* (Philadelphia, PA: Fortress, 1978), Ch. 3 & 4.

14. See R. J. Starratt, 'The Prophetic Education Leader', *Religion and Education*, 24, 1, 1997, pp.40-45.

15. See K. Scott, op.cit.

16. T. Groome, *Christian Religious Education* (New Year: Harper and Row, 1980) and Sharing Faith (New York, Harper and Row, 1991).

17. See N. C. Burbules and S. Rice, 'Dialogue across Differences: Continuing a Conversation', *Harvard Educational Review*, 61, 4, 1991, pp.393-416.

18. See C. Melchert, *Wise Teaching: Biblical Wisdom and Educational Ministry*, (Harrisburg, PA: Trinity Press International, 1998) and 'Pluralistic Religious Education in a Postmodern World', *Religion Education* 90 pp.3,4, 1995: 346-359; 'Wisdom is Vindicated by Her Deeds', *Religious Education* 87, 1, 1992, pp.127-151.

19. See G. Moran, *Interplay: A Theory of Religion and Education* (Winona: St Mary's Press, 1981): *Religious Education Development: Images for the Future* (Minneapolis: Winston Press, 1983); *Religious Education as a Second Language*, op.cit. and M. Harris and G. Moran, *Reshaping Religious Education: Conversations on Contemporary Practice* (Louisville, KY: Westminster John Knox, 1998).

Chapter 5

Practising the Trinity in the Local Church: The Symbol as Icon and Lure

KIERAN SCOTT

This chapter explores the task of teaching people to be religious through a post-modern reinterpretation of the classic doctrine of the Trinity. For the Christian, to know God is to live trinitarian. Living in a trinitarian way, however, can be understood in two senses: as *orthodoxy*, as correct believing, as the right perception of God as revealed in Jesus of Nazareth, and, as *orthopraxis*, as right practice, as living out this perception in right acts. The Christian doctrine of the Trinity is orthodoxy (right perception), and it calls for orthopraxis (right response). In both of these meanings, the doctrine is eminently practical. It emerges as the theological criterion to measure the faithfulness of the practices of the local church – its ethics, spirituality and worship. It can have far-reaching consequences for Christian living. This is the thesis I wish to pursue in this chapter.

On first impressions, the thesis may seem overextended or exaggerated. In Christian communities, most consent to the doctrine in theory but have little need for it in their religious practice. The doctrine has the reputation of being an arcane and abstract theory that has no relevance to Christian practice. It has been relegated to the margins of the tradition, vexed theologians, puzzled preachers on Trinity Sunday, and frustrated parish religious educators. In fact, the late Karl

Rahner once remarked that even if one could show the doctrine of the Trinity to be false, the major part of Christian literature could well remain virtually unchanged. So detached has the triune symbol become from the actual religious life of most people, he noted, that if people were to read in their morning newspapers that a fourth person of the Trinity had been discovered it would cause little stir or at least less than a typical Vatican pronouncement on sexual matters.[1]

But this was not always the case. In the fourth century, Gregory of Nyssa complained that one could not go into the marketplace to exchange money, buy bread, or go to the baths, without getting involved in a discussion about whether God the Son is equal to or less than God the Father. Gregory wondered whether this enthusiasm for divine discourse was the result of perversity, delirium or intellectual derangement. These lively debates in the public square on the Trinity would be hard to imagine today. This pre-modern doctrine is at the periphery of modern religious consciousness, and has become unintelligible and religiously irrelevant on a vast scale. And, yet, we cannot do without a trinitarian doctrine of God. It articulates the heart of the Christian tradition. The doctrine, potentially, offers a theoretical framework that yields a wisdom, a discernment, a guide to practising the Body of Christ, to being the Body of Christ in the world.

But why has the doctrine been neglected, evaded and appeared so esoteric that one could well do without it? This demise of the Trinity must be understood before it can be rejuvenated for postmodern culture and ecclesial praxis. My argument is developed in a four-step process of exploration and discussion:

1. The God symbol: What's at stake?
2. The denouement of the Trinity;
3. Theological retrieval: Letting the symbol sing again;
4. The Trinity as a principle of action in the local church.

My assumption is: the doctrine of the Trinity, hermeneutically revitalised, is bound up with every dimension of the divine-human relationship. It is a heuristic framework for thinking correctly about God, and us in relation to God. In that sense, there is no doctrine as practical or that has such profound consequences for congregational living.

1. The God Symbol: What's at Stake?

In a religious context, a symbol is a word or an image that participates in the reality it points to. The symbol opens up some understanding of that reality, but never fully exhausts it. God is such a symbol for Christians. The word points toward inexhaustible mystery and, yet, allows us 'to see through a glass darkly'.

The symbol of God is at the centre of the Christian tradition. It functions as the primary symbol of the whole religious system. And, like every symbol, it has evocative power. It is the ultimate reference point for the values of a community. 'The symbol of God', Elizabeth Johnson writes, 'represents what the community takes to be its highest good, its most profound truth, its most appealing beauty. It is the ultimate point for understanding personal experience, social life, and the world as a whole. In turn, the symbol of God powerfully molds the corporate identity of the community, highlights its values, and directs its praxis'.[2] How the symbol functions, then, seems crucial. And, a great deal seems at stake in what values and visions it evokes.

Gordon Kaufman, in *The Theological Imagination: Constructing the Concept of God*, deduces some examples from the above premise. A religion, he notes, that would worship a warlike God and extol the way he smashes his enemies to bits, would promote aggressive and hostile behaviour as religious. A community that would acclaim God as an arbitrary tyrant would inspire its members to acts of impatience and disrespect toward their fellow creatures.[3] Continuing this line of deduction, Kaufman, in his *Theology for a Nuclear Age*, claims a religious body that promotes a sovereign God, where God acting as king fights on the side of his chosen ones to bring their enemies down, risks endangering the planet with nuclear annihilation.[4] Sallie McFague, in her *Models of God: Theology for an Ecological Nuclear Age*, demonstrates the destructive ecological implications of a hierarchical, imperialistic and detached God.[5]

On the other hand, Kaufman and McFague show that the symbol of God can function in a very different way. Their constructive theological projects re-image a God appropriate to our post-modern time. A community that acclaims a beneficent and loving God who forgives offenses would turn the religious community toward care for the neighbour and mutual forgiveness. A religion that speaks of a relational God involved in the network of human and non-human relations inspires mutuality among people and care for the world as God's body. And, as feminist theologians have pushed to the forefront of our consciousness, when our religious discourse names God in female and male terms, patriarchy and exclusion is challenged and an inclusive communal vision emerges.

The symbol of God, then, shapes the life orientation of the faith community and guides its individual members. The symbol evokes our ultimate concerns. It is what our heart clings to most deeply and what we give our heart to most passionately. The holy mystery that the symbol represents undergirds the principles, choices, values and relationships of the communal body. As a symbol, it is never neutral or abstract. Rather it functions, for better or worse, to unify and express the community's worldview, its expectation of design and order for the world, and its foundational orientation to human life.

But we can legitimately ask: what determines how the symbol functions? The simple answer is: the way we talk about God. That is, the images and metaphors we attach to the symbol. In the Christian tradition, there is a right (orthodox) way and a wrong (unorthodox) way to speak about God. *The specific Christian way of speaking about God is in trinitarian terms.* This is crucial to its perception of reality, and it emerges from the Christian people's deepest intuitions and feelings. The Christian God is a trinitarian icon. Historically, this triune icon has functioned ambiguously in Christian communities. For an extensive period in Christian history, the Trinity suggested a God isolated from, and absolute ruler of, human affairs. In contrast, in an earlier period, the symbol of the Trinity represented the indwelling of God, as a three-fold *koinonia*, in history. The latter functioned to call forth loving relationships in the community and in the world as the highest good. Positively, this understanding of the Trinity modeled the ideal of sacrificial love and service (*agape*) in relations. Negatively, it prophetically challenged social and ecological injustices. Here, the triune God is love, and empowers mutuality, equality and inclusiveness in relations. In this hermeneutical understanding, wherever hearts are healed, justice done, liberation breaks forth and the earth flourishes, there the human and non-human community reflects, in part, the trinitarian God. But this understanding of the Trinity has not functioned for the last thousand years in the West.

2. The Denouement of the Trinity

Catherine LaCugna offers the striking metaphor of 'defeat' regarding the downfall of the doctrine of the Trinity in recent centuries. The doctrine, she writes, has been neglected, literalised, treated like a fringe curiosity or analysed with conceptual acrobatics completely inappropriate to its meaning.[6] LaCugna's work brilliantly traces the emergence and defeat of the doctrine of the Trinity, and its decline into becoming something hidden and esoteric. Her work chronicles the historical roots of the problem, but also attends to the contemporary challenge feminist theology poses to the doctrine. Appreciation of trinitarian speech about God has lessened, LaCugna argues, due to two main factors: the doctrine loosing its mooring in experience, and feminist critique of the symbol as sustaining patriarchy. She addresses these two distinct but interrelated causes.

Loss of Mooring in Experience

Trinitarian images, concepts and patterns existed from the first century in the sacred writings, liturgy and confessional statements of Christians. No doctrine of the Trinity per se, however, existed until the fourth century. The doctrine emerged in response to the Arian controversy. The early Church from its origins struggled to interpret the meaning of the gospel. A set of difficult questions confronted it: How was the Jesus movement in continuity with Judaism? What was the role of Jesus in salvation? Is he the mediator of salvation? Who saves us? Is it God? Jesus? The Holy Spirit? Is Jesus on a par with God or less than God? In the early 300s, these questions reached a feverish pitch. Arius, a priest from Alexandria, vigorously maintained that God (the Father) is absolutely unique and transcendent. God's essence cannot be shared by another or transferred to another (such as the Son). The difference between Father and Son was one of substance. For Arius, then, Jesus was 'less than God' – greater, perhaps, than the rest of us, but still less than God. This view of Arius was officially condemned at the Council of Nicaea (325). Nicaea affirmed that Jesus is on a par with God, 'of the same nature' as God, divine as well as fully human. Arius could not imagine God submitting Godself to the vicissitudes of time and matter. This was his basic heresy. But from the debate and controversy the doctrine of the Trinity was born.

This, however, did not settle matters. Not until the Council of Constantinople in 381 would there be an official pronouncement that the Spirit is God. But how do we explain Father, Son and Spirit as God? After Nicaea, theological explanations were given in philosophical terms. Arius pushed theology toward ontology. The Cappodocian Fathers, Basil (d.379), Gregory of Nyssa (d.394), and Gregory of Nazianzus (d. 390) formulated the Trinitarian doctrine in its classic form: God is one nature, three persons. This Greek theology had a dynamic understanding of God. We cannot know what God is, but we know God from God's 'operations' or 'energies'. When the Cappodocians wrote about the relation of the Father, Son and Holy Spirit to each other, they always had in mind the divine persons in the economy of salvation. God is unimaginably severed from the world or divorced from the redemptive work of Jesus. Athanasius (d.373) captures this in his well-known statement: 'God became human that we might become God'.

In the Latin west, however, trinitarian theology took a very different trajectory. This metaphysical approach starts with the one divine substance, the 'Godhead' that the three divine persons share in common. With Augustine (d.430) leading the way, Latin trinitarian theology emphasises divine nature rather than divine persons. It became an exploration of God in Godself in an eternal, intra-divine realm, in contrast to, God for us in the economy of salvation. In technical terms, it was a shift from Trinity *pro nobis* to Trinity *in se*. Augustine pursued his argument employing psychological analogies. The internal workings of the human being, he wrote, analogically correspond to the internal life of God. Augustine's perspective would win the day and influence trinitarian theology for a millennium. However, it was a pyrrhic victory. The doctrine lost its footing in the concrete details of salvation history, severed its connection to religious experience and became remote from practices of congregational life.

The focus was now on God's 'inner' life. The key question became: how are Father, Son and Spirit related to each other? The image we get is of a 'heavenly committee' of persons enclosed in a circle or arranged in a vertical row. It is as if God is sighted through a high-powered telescope and the internal interactions of the three persons are intended to be taken literally. In Karl Rahner's phrase, God is viewed as a Trinity, 'absolutely locked up within itself' and does not touch our lives.[7] Trinitarian theology now became abstract, impractical, ahistorical, and immune to the concerns of ecclesial, spiritual and liturgical life. In a word, the symbol became divorced from the life-giving experiences that gave it birth in human understanding. For LaCugna, this was the defeat of the Trinity.

Feminist Theological Critique
To add to the trinitarian woes stated above, contemporary feminist theology has confronted the classic doctrine of the Trinity with a set of additional problems. It is seen as a stumbling block to the concerns of Christian feminism by sustaining the patriarchal subordination of women. In an effort to counteract this, the symbol is critiqued on two fronts: its male imagery and the hierarchical pattern of divine relationships.

God is named Father, Son and Spirit in the doctrine of the Trinity. This exclusive male imagery is the first difficulty feminists face. It reinforces the assumption of a male God within a monarchical framework. The symbol points implicitly to an essential divine maleness. The male is *imago Dei*. The same cannot be said for the female. This exclusive focus on masculine images pervades theology, liturgy and catechesis. It has functioned to cast men into superior roles and women into dependent ones. In a word, it has given religious legitimation to patriarchy.

Elizabeth Johnson challenges this male hegemony and embarks on a reconstruction of the doctrine of the Trinity intentionally using only female metaphors.[8] Sallie McFague points out that the problem is not that God is imaged as Father, but that Fatherhood has become the root metaphor for God. Her trinitarian reconstruction names God as Mother, Lover and Friend.[9] Some critics see her proposal as more unitarian than trinitarian. Catherine LaCugna cautions us, however, not to be like Arius. Arius, it has been said, did not know a metaphor when he saw one. La Cugna reminds us of the propensity to literalise metaphors for God and to forget the dissimilarity in every analogy. The Father-Son analogy is simply that, an analogy. Any analogy. she notes, would have sufficed if it expressed relationship between persons of the same nature (for example Mother-Daughter, Father-Daughter, Mother-Son). The Father-Son analogy emerged naturally at the time. It communicated that God is personal and that equality existed between Father and Son. Rather than concede that God the Father is male as patriarchy defined it, the opposite claim is made. This is a God of mutuality, equality and inclusiveness. 'One can affirm the doctrine of the Trinity', writes LaCugna, 'and also use the metaphors of Father and Son, without consenting that God is male'.[10] Trinitarian theology, then, is not inherently sexist and patriarchal. The doctrine of the Trinity envisions a relational God of love, mutuality, self-giving and self-receiving. Ironically, these values are the leitmotif of Christian feminism.

The second objection raised by feminist theology is the hierarchical pattern of divine relations. This seems to compromise the feminist concern for equality among women and men. In the trinitarian schema, the first person is the principle and originating source of divinity itself. The Son and Spirit emanate from the Father. Such a model carries an implicit subordination. Elizabeth Johnson argues, 'When the model used... focuses on the procession of first to second to third, a subtle hierarchy is set up and, like a drowned continent, bends all currents of trinitarian thought to the shape of the model used. Through insistence on the right order of certain processions, ontological priority inevitably ends up with the Father while at the other end of the procession the Spirit barely trails along'.[11] The basic metaphor, she notes signifies an order of precedence. In spite of a built-in corrective in the classical model that insists on the radical equality of the three persons, Johnson claims the image falters and is not capable of bearing the burden of mutuality. 'Different metaphor systems are needed', she writes, 'to show the equality, mutuality, and reciprocal dynamism of trinitarian relation'.[12] This is the project she embarks on in *She Who Is: The Mystery of God in Feminist Theological Discourse.*

Catherine LaCugna has empathy with Johnson's project. On the other hand, she cautions against slipping into a debate about 'intra divine' equality. Fundamentally, the Trinity is not an account of God's self-relatedness. Its chief concern is not how Father, Son and Spirit are related to each other, but how the triune mystery is related to us. The genius of the Cappodocians was to assert that Godhead originates in personhood. Personhood is being-in-relation-to-another, someone toward another. This is the ultimate organising principle of reality. The title Father simply means the essential relational and personal nature of God. There is no primacy of one person over another. 'Trinitarian monotheism', LaCugna writes, 'preserved the principle of shared rule and banished once and for all – at least theoretically – the idea that any person can be subordinate to another'.[13]

Furthermore, she warns feminism against the temptation of projecting onto an intra-divine realm its vision of what it hopes would happen in the human sphere.[14] This could leave feminism defenseless against the charge of ideological imposition, and methodologically tie it to the wrong starting point and end point, namely, God's inner relatedness. The doctrinal trinitarian God, on the other hand, is God for us. There are not two sets of communion – one among the divine persons, the other among human persons. The God of the Trinity dwells among us in communion. Hierarchy is found to be unorthodox. Feminist theology can resonate with these sensibilities. The defeat of the Trinity, then, does not rest at the feet of feminism. Ironically, however, its re-emergence and revitalisation is, in part, the fruit of contemporary feminist wisdom.

3. Theological Retrieval: Letting the Symbol Sing Again.

Initially, the various and serious challenges to the classic doctrine of the Trinity seem to threaten a foundational Christian symbol. The critiques, however, may in Bonhoffer's words, be a providential clearing of the deck so that the relational Christian God can be rediscovered. Striking creative and imaginative efforts have been underway to do just that. The efforts at retrieval have involved three distinct but related tasks. This work has revolved around: 1) re-rooting the Trinity in the experience of salvation, 2) re-discovering the metaphorical nature of trinitarian speech, and, 3) re-connecting the symbol to thoughtful practice (praxis). I will proceed, in turn, to explain each of these tasks.

Re-rooting the Trinity in the Experience of Salvation
Catherine LaCugna draws our attention to an icon of the Trinity painted by the fifteenth century Russian artist Andrei Rublev.[15] The icon is inspired by the story of Genesis 18. It depicts three angels seated around a table on which there is a eucharistic cup. In the background is a house and a tree. Genesis 18 tells a story of extraordinary hospitality. Three strangers arrive at the home of Abraham and Sarah. They are invited into their household to share their resources. Sarah baked bread and Abraham prepared the meal. During the meal, the strangers offer their hosts the pledge of a child who will carry on the promise. In Rublev's icon, Abraham and Sarah's home is transformed into a temple, the dwelling place of God. The oak tree stands for the tree of life. The position of the three figures is very suggestive. They are arranged in a circle inclining toward one another but the circle is not closed. Intuitively, there is a sense that one is not only invited into the (triune) circle, but that one is already part of it.

Rublev's trinitarian imagery suggests that the mystery of God is not a self-contained God, or a closed divine society. The archetype is of hospitality. The image is a communion in relationship. The triune figures invite the world to join the feast. The divine communion is loving, open to the world and seeks its nourishment. And the eucharistic cup in the center is the sacramental sign of our communion with God and with each other. LaCugna observes, 'This icon expresses the fundamental insight of the doctrine of the Trinity, namely, that God is not far from us but lives among us in a community of persons'.[16] This seminal insight LaCugna retrieves from the Cappodocian fathers.

Today trinitarian theology is being creatively and fruitfully recovered. This is due in part to the rising interest in liturgy, spirituality, world religions, and the attempt to find a solid theological basis for praxis. Reclaiming the wisdom of the Cappodocians resonates with postmodern sensibilities and lays the groundwork for revitalising the doctrine. The first task in this revitalisation is to root the Trinity in the experience of salvation.

All religious doctrine springs from an encounter or experience with God. This is also true of the Trinity. It is a symbol that developed historically out of the religious experience of a people. The early Christians came to see that their encounter with Jesus of Nazareth was nothing less than divine. Salvation has been offered to them in his ministry. But, after his death and resurrection, they continued to experience his saving grace through the presence and activity of the Spirit in the community. For them, God was utterly transcendent. On the other hand, they could sense God's spirit in their communal experience. In other words, they experienced the saving God in a threefold manner, as beyond them, with them, and within them. Consequently, they began to express their idea of God in this (trinitarian) pattern. Salvation came from God (the Father) through Jesus (the Son) in the Holy Spirit. With this articulation, the Christian conception of God as Trinity was born. But it was born from their religious experience, and inextricably linked to the saving work of Jesus. The Christian

God is liberating in history. The mystery is not an isolated monad, but a living communion in relation with the world. This is a God to us and for us. It was the genius of the Cappodocians – Basil, Gregory of Nyssa and Gregory of Nazianzus – to imaginatively capture this profound truth in terms rooted in human experience.

The initial concern of the Cappodocians was with our salvation, not with metaphysics. Consequently, the economy of salvation is the basis, the context, and the final criterion for every statement they make about God. The Cappodocians made person rather than substance their primary ontological category. This radical move asserts that God is personal, not impersonal. Father, Son and Spirit are relational terms indicating God's relation to us. A person is a being-in-relation-to-another. The essence of God is to be in relationship to other persons. This triune mystery of persons in communal relations points to the life-giving nature of divine life. God by nature is outgoing love and self donation. As LaCugna notes, 'If God were not personal, God would not exist at all'.[17] The Trinity, then, is a theology of relationship. The symbol reveals truth about the mystery of God, and reveals us to ourselves. To be is to be in (personal) relations. God reveals Godself in the depths of relationality. This was the God revealed in the salvific work of Jesus of Nazareth. And, it is the same Spirit of God revealed in our salvific Christ-like relations today. At this point, the doctrine of the Trinity becomes meaningful again. It is re-rooted in personal experience from which it first sprung.

Re-discovering the Metaphorical Nature of Trinitarian Speech
The second task in revitalising the doctrine of the Trinity is a renewed appreciation for the doctrine of analogy. Traditionally, the doctrine of analogy was meant to provide a way of speaking of God which allows for both similarity and difference between God and the human. It became a sensitive and indirect way to speak about God. All our religious language is

analogical or metaphorical. A metaphor contains an 'is' and an 'is not': God is and is not like a father, mother, spouse. The linguistic tension in the metaphor forces the mind to seek meaning at a deeper level. A literalised metaphor, however, paralyses the imagination. When we literalise God metaphors, we create an idol. We assimilate God to human categories. Theological feminism is in part a critique of our propensity to literalise metaphors for God. Frequently, our discourse on the Trinity is conducted in implicit literal and descriptive language. This shows up in the key notion of person and the number one and three.

In the trinitarian doctrine, person is symbolic language. It is not intended to be taken literally. There are not three distinct somebodies, with three distinct centres of consciousness. This is tritheism. Person refers to God only indirectly, metaphorically. Person indicates relationship, freedom, and the capacity to love and be loved, to know and be known, to be distinct, but connected. The concept person reminds us that no metaphor is adequate to name the mystery. This is the case also for the numbers one and three.

The words one and three seem to stand for mathematical quantities. But this is not the intent of the doctrinal language. The words do not refer to numbers in the usual sense. The language is analogical. Elizabeth Johnson writes, 'To say that God is one is intended to negate division, thus affirming the unity of divine being. To say that the persons are three is intended to negate singleness, thus affirming a communion in God'.[18] God is at one with Godself and, simultaneously, in communion with the world. God is not a mind bending mathematical puzzle but a one God who is disclosed in communal relation. Trinitarian speech, then is metaphorical. It is like a finger pointing to the moon (Augustine). It ought not to be confused with the moon. When we rediscover the allusive character of this speech, the doctrine comes alive.

Re-Connecting the Symbol to Thoughtful Practice
The third task in revitalising the Trinity is to link doctrinal orthodoxy with correct religious practice, namely, orthopraxis. As Paul Ricoeur notes, the symbol gives rise to thought. It has an evocative power that calls for a response. In other words, the symbol functions. Likewise, a creative retrieval of the trinitarian symbol also functions. It calls for a right response. The symbol is an icon that lures toward thoughtful religious practice. The (symbolic) doctrine suggests living. And, in light of the retrieval noted above, living out the doctrine amounts to living God's life with one another. No separation can exist between the content of the doctrine and the essential acts of believers. Correct perception is inseparable from correct practice. To believe in a trinitarian way gives rise to trinitarian living, that is, it evokes a moral response. This guarantees that the Christian doctrine of God is intrinsically connected to every dimension of life where God and creature live together. It is, then, immensely practical. This is what the doctrine has been cut off from during its defeat. With its revitalisation, however, it grounds our Christian praxis. In a word, it entails living as Jesus did. The implications of this trinitarian discipleship are the subject of the final part of this chapter.

4. The Trinity as a Principle of Action in the Local Church
From the beginning Christians confessed and prayed to God the Father, through Jesus Christ in the Holy Spirit. This confession and pattern of prayer signaled a new religious identity. It meant the Church's life to mirror God's life. It is to be an 'icon' of God. In its corporate life, its structures and practices, it is to embody the nature of God. In other words, it is to practise the Trinity (or, in the words of Paul, be the Body of Christ). Principles can be gleaned from the Christian doctrine of the Trinity and applied to the ethical, spiritual, political and educational life of the church. The implications can be transformative and the consequences radical for Christian practice. We can now take

up this theoretical framework of the Trinity and see how it yields a wisdom and can act as a guide for Christian living.

Ethical Transformation

A trinitarian theology of God is the proper theological basis for Christian ethics. Ethics pertains to right actions of persons. Humanity is created in the image of God, and God exists as a personal communion of love. The very essence of God is to be in relations. The symbol indicates also the particular kind of relatedness: one of genuine mutuality in which there is radical equality while distinctions are respected. The symbol functions. It evokes a moral life of a reciprocal exchange of love. We are called to be persons: being from and for others. This trinitarian ethic contains within it a critical principle that can act as a prophetic protest against the individualistic and utilitarian ethic of today. To be fully a person is to be personal, communal, self-giving and self-receiving. A solitary, impersonal, self-centered life is morally unnatural. It is unorthodox. Orthopraxis is right actions for persons. It consists of everything that supports and promotes the flourishing of persons. Whatever promotes communion amid diversity and strife, whatever enables us to live a life of virtue, whatever cultivates habitual practices of compassion and care, whatever frees us from narcissism and making idols of things – these are the staples of a trinitarian moral life.

Trinitarian ethics, however, is not generic but Christological. The proper context for its discussion and discernment is the economy of salvation. Jesus is the embodied face of God for Christians. And a key criterion for Christian understanding of divine mystery lies in Jesus' preaching of the reign of God. The God whom Jesus preached is in solidarity with the slave, the sinner, the poor, the marginalised and with the least of persons. Followers of Jesus the Christ are exhorted to be icons of Christ. He is the criterion of what we are to become. In Christ, divine love is to be inclusive, healing and uniting. The 'God brought low' in Jesus is the God whose face is seen in the poor, the oppressed, the other, not in the rich, the powerful and the privileged. When we are Christ to each other, the reign of God is made present for the transformation of the world.

This moral vision cannot forecast programmatic remedies for elitism, materialism or sexism. And we should avoid the temptation of projecting our own social or political ideology onto the 'inner' life of God. However, the doctrine of the Trinity does contain moral insights that can function as a critical principle against all nontrinitarian forms of life and evokes a creative alternative vision of a transformed moral order. Political and liberation theologies today rightly perceive that a doctrine of God cannot be unrelated to the specific ethical, economic and political demands of the Christian life.[19] Feminist theologies have tapped into the doctrinal vision for a reshaping of the pattern of human/ecological relations and for a reconstructing of a sexual ethic.[20] Christian social ethicists find in the trinitarian doctrine a framework for grounding the discussion of human rights in a communal context.[21] And, ecclesiologists elicit from the symbol a vision of the Church's social mission.[22] In short, ethical life means walking in the ways of God, walking in a transformed, Christ-like manner.

Spiritual Transformation
Spirituality is undergoing a widespread renaissance today. The interest in it is phenomenal and touches multiple levels in our society. The new literature attempts to respond to the deep yearnings of contemporary men and women. There is a hunger, a quest beyond materiality. There is also a deeply felt need to overcome the fragmentation of modern life. The 'new spirituality' holds the promise of healing the world's splits.

There is a danger, however, in some of the new spiritualities. There is a premature jump into unity with high-level generalities and abstractions. The orientation lends itself to a Disneyland or cafeteria-style choosing, a fuzzy concern and love for the whole world, but for no one in particular. This popularised spiritual quest is tailored to the individual's privatised needs and desires. It is shaped by consumer impulses and captive to a therapeutic culture. It is as if we can save ourselves by ourselves if we would turn toward developing our own spiritual centre. This is a privatised and rootless spirituality. Frequently, it is in reaction against organised religion and detached from its disciplined practices. Trinitarian spirituality, however, takes a dramatically different form.

Spiritual life means being animated by the Spirit of God. It means participating in the very life of God. It is a process of 'deification'. Specifically, in a Christian context, life in the Spirit is life in Christ. It is becoming like Christ ('ingodded' or 'Christified'). This 'deification' of the human person involves modeling trinitarian life. It involves boundless self-giving, pouring out love for the sake of life. It creates inclusive community among persons and helps bring about the reign of God.

Trinitarian spirituality, then, is incarnational. It is rooted in the practice of everyday life. It is a style of life, a way of being in the world in light of the Mystery. Holiness is becoming whole, being perfected as a human being. And, the imitation of Christ means fulfilling this vocation. The saints among us are those who answer this call and convert to this way. This is a personal and communal spirituality. It is concerned with a right response to the non-human universe. It has justice at its center. Here there is no split between the contemplative and the active. They are a rhythm in one's life. And, this rhythm will centre our lives and help us find peace. In other words, we will be transformed.

Political Transformation
While the doctrine of the Trinity is the product of patriarchal culture, its hermeneutical rejuvenation allows it to function as a protest against patriarchal governance. It can be the basis for

trinitarian ecclesiology. While many members of the ecclesial body have experienced its life as exclusive, discriminating, unjust and oppressive, the symbol does provide the critical principle against which we can measure present institutional arrangement.

The doctrine reminds us that the arch or rule of God is the arch of love and communion among persons. Among the three there is no domination and subordination, no first and last. In God there is neither hierarchy nor inequality, neither division nor competition, but only unity in love amid diversity.

The Christian community is to mirror this inclusivity and reciprocal power. It is simply unorthodox to claim subordination in ecclesial government. The symbol calls us to a community of equal discipleship, a kinship of sisterhood and brotherhood, equal partners in mutual relations. When we are baptised into the community, we acquire a new identity. Previous patterns of relationship are reordered. We 'put on Christ' (Gal. 3:27). Alienating patterns of domination and division are thrown off. We are reborn into new life. Patriarchal power dies and is transformed into emancipatory communal empowerment.

The doctrine of the Trinity does not specify the exact forms of structure and community appropriate to the Church. However, it does evoke our questioning. As Catherine LaCugna notes, it suggests, 'we may ask whether our institutions, rituals, and administrative practices foster elitism, discrimination, competition... or whether the church is run like God's household: a domain of inclusiveness, interdependence, and cooperation'.[23] Like Rublev's icon, the Church is called to be a trinitarian sign of love and reciprocity. Only a community of profound mutuality of power corresponds to the triune symbol.

Educational Transformation
Finally, a legitimate claim can be made that the Trinity ought to

form the basis of the Church's educational practices. It is not overextending the symbol to relate it to educational ministry. This can be done briefly in two ways:

1. Attending to educational design
2. Pedagogical processes.

Education begins with creation of design, or more accurately, reshaping the present design. Educational life forms already come formed. The best the teacher can do is work with learners and environment to improve the given design. The term 'design', Gabriel Moran writes, 'attempts to capture both the express intent of the human teacher and the material limits of what can be taught'.[24] The student enters an already formed physical environment. For change or learning to take place, this involves the reshaping of the human organism in relation to its environment. To teach, then, is to show how this is done. It requires changing the existing design that relates the person's activity and the environment.

What does this mean for educational ministry? The answer seems logical: education in the church begins with the creation of trinitarian designs. The teacher's task is to give God-like shape to educational space. This involves fashioning an aesthetic, communal environment that evokes transformation. By re-designing ecclesial learning environments in trinitarian patterns, we refashion the people of God.

The Trinity can also be an icon for pedagogical processes in the Church. The symbol gives rise to thoughtful conversation. Students are invited into a relationship of mutuality, equality and reciprocity. Depositing knowledge or beliefs into 'empty' heads is unorthodox. Knowledge and interpretations are socially constructed. The dialogue honours solidarity, diversity and the otherness of the written texts and human texts. Teaching is from and for others. It is vocational work. The Church teacher is the guardian of the tradition. If this custodial work is done in a trinitarian manner, the tradition can flower into richer meaning. It will be transformed.

The thesis of this chapter is that the central theme of the doctrine of the Trinity is relationship: God's relationship with us and our relationship with one another. The symbol articulates our understanding of 'right relationship'. The doctrine is a reminder that the trinitarian God is an icon of the local church. The symbol is a lure to practise the reign of God. This is the triumph of the Trinity.

Notes

1. K. Rahner, *The Trinity* (New York: Herder and Herder, 1970).
2. E. Johnson, 'Trinity: To Let the Symbol Sing Again', *Theology Today* 54(3), p. 299-311.
3. G. Kaufman, *The Theological Imagination: Constructing the Concept of God* (Philadelphia: Westminster, 1981) p. 187-189.
4. G. Kaufman, *Theology for a Nuclear Age* (Philadelphia: Westminster, 1985).
5. Sallie McFague, *Models of God: Theology for an Ecological, Nuclear Age* (Philadelphia: Fortress, 1987).
6. Catherine LaCugna, *God for Us: The Trinity and Christian Life* (San Francisco: Harper, 1991a). *The Trinitarian Mystery of God. Systematic Theology: Roman Catholic Perspectives*, ed. Francis S. Fiorenza and John P. Galvin (Minneapolis: Fortress, 1,149-91, 1991b).
7. K. Rahner, *The Trinity*.
8. Elizabeth Johnson, *She Who Is: The Mystery of God in Feminist Theological Discourse* (New York: Crossroads, 1992).
9. Sallie McFague, op cit.
10. C. LaCugna, op cit, p. 182.
11. E. Johnson, op cit, p. 196.
12. Ibid p. 197.
13. C. LaCugna, *God in Communion with Us. Freeing Theology: The Essentials of Theology in Feminist Perspective*, ed. C.M. LaCugna (San Francisco: Harper, p. 83-114, 1993).
14. C. LaCugna, op cit (1991a).
15. C. LaCugna, op cit (1993).

16. C. LaCugna, op cit, p. 84 (1993).
17. C. LaCugna, ibid, p. 87.
18. E. Johnson, op cit, p. 204.
19. A. Hunt, *What Are They Saying About the Trinity?* (Mahwah: Paulist Press, 1998).
20. C. LaCugna, *Making the Most of Trinity Sunday. Worship* 60, pp. 210-224 (1986). E. Johnson, op cit (1992).
21. M.J. Himes and K.R. Himes, *The Trinity and Human Rights. Fullness of Faith: The Public significance of Theology* (Mahwah: Paulist Press, 1993) pp. 55-73.
22. J.H. Sanks, *The Social Mission of the Church: Its Changing Context.* Lowaim Studies, 25, pp. 23-48.
23. C. LaCugna, op cit p. 402 (1991).
24. Gabriel Moran, *Showing How: The Act of Teaching* (Valley Forge: Trinity pp. 59-79, 1997).

EPILOGUE

If one accepts that culture is an active system that produces meaning it becomes clear that when culture changes radically, meanings and values change radically; for example, the consumerist dimension of contemporary culture is very deep and penetrating and not simply an outer frame that surrounds people's lives. In the words of John O'Donohue, 'it is a way of thinking which seeps into our minds and becomes a powerful inner compass. Consumerism leaves us marooned in a cul-de-sac of demented longing, helpless targets of its relentless multiplication.' He goes on to say that consumerism is the new religion or in parallel fashion quantity is the new divinity: 'The power of this divinity is its ability to reach you anywhere'.[1]

Since contemporary culture is so deep and penetrating it behoves educators, and in particular religious educators, to become involved in what Michael Warren describes as 'cultural agency' and re-imagine the world of all age groups, particularly the young. One of the most effective ways of re-imagining the world is through the medium of authentic religious education. All balanced and healthy spirituality derives from the quality and power of the imagination. There is no more worthy religious imagination of life to offer people than that based on the biblical metaphor of the reign of God, at least in the

Christian tradition. One recognises that this is not an easy task because of the tension between authentic religious culture and lived post-modern culture. While the tension between Christ and Culture has been a perennial one it is especially difficult in contemporary western culture to successfully impart and maintain the vision of Jesus, since social status, success and domination are highly valued and continually reinforced in electronic narratives and daily living. This is not to say that there is a total clash between religion and culture, as only certain features of the religious and secular signifying systems clash with each other. Indeed, there are many positive, humanising elements in the secular culture and, as was pointed out in Chapter One, post-modernity is characterised by a new search for, and openness to, the mystical, the spiritual and to community.

Our perennial search for meaning continues and one of the tasks of the religious educator is to accompany people on that search and to enable them to use their religious vision as a lens through which culture can be viewed and evaluated. Warren describes this as educating people:

> First to think about how meaning is created, in whose interests it is created and what sort of rendition of reality is it; and the ability, second, to make judgements about the meaning presented to us, using aesthetic, ideological and religious criteria.[2]

Chapters Two and Three of this book have made a strong case for the teaching of religion – an activity that is central to human life. Religious education has two clear aims: (a) to teach religion in a thoroughly intellectual manner based on sound educational principles; (b) to teach people to be religious in their way of being and way of life. If one aim is focused upon to the detriment of the other, an imbalance creeps in which can lead to dangerous consequences. This is particularly true if the intellectual and critical is downgraded. John O'Donohue points out that 'Most of the time we are not even aware of how our thinking encircles everything' and 'when we wake up to how our thoughts create our world, we become conscious of the ways in which we can be blind and limited'.[3] This points to the importance of giving balanced attention to both aims of religious education as it does to the importance of complementing schooling with other diverse forms of religiously educative activities attended to in Chapter Four. The parish is one indispensable location for the actualising of one of the aims of religious education, namely, teaching people to be religious. Revitalised Christian doctrines can show the way as was illustrated in Chapter Five.

All religious traditions attend to the nurturing of both their young and adult members into the religious way of life. Consequently, this aim of religious education is unlikely to be neglected. The danger is that the other aim might not receive sufficient attention at a time when religious critique is so necessary in today's world culture. Religious education should enable people to critique their own religious culture as well as the wider culture which they inhabit. This should enable them to become less 'blind and limited' in their human and religious perception of reality.

It is important to challenge the widely held assumption that religion, by its very nature, is good or indeed that a religious attitude to life is always praiseworthy. After all, it was religious people who instigated the Crusades and instituted the Inquisition in the Middle Ages under the leadership of Pope Gregory IX in 1233. In 1649 it was a group of leading clergy who drew up a confession of faith, later to become the doctrinal statements of the Church of Scotland and the Presbyterian Church of Ireland which – incredible as it sounds to us today – included a sentence referring to the Pope as 'that anti-Christ'. It was religious fundamentalists who crashed planes into New York's twin towers, into the

Pentagon and in Pennsylvania killing thousands of people on 11 September 2001. Religion continues to be a major factor in many conflicts around the world today, whether it be fundamentalist Christianity or fundamentalist Islam, whether it be in Northern Ireland, the United States, Iraq, Afghanistan or the Middle East.

Critique of religion is of perennial importance, indeed, never more so than in our contemporary world culture. Authentic religious education will of its nature attend to this if the two aims of religious education outlined in this book continue to be explored and developed.

Oliver Brennan

1 February 2005

Notes

1. J. O'Donohue, *Eternal Echoes: Exploring the Hunger to Belong* (Bantam Press, 1998) p.80.
2. Quoted in O.Brennan, *Cultures Apart* p. 157.
3. *Eternal Echoes*, p.83.
4. Ibid, p.204.